WILD SOCIALISM

*Workers Councils in Revolutionary Berlin,
1918–21*

Martin Comack

University Press of America,® Inc.
Lanham · Boulder · New York · Toronto · Plymouth, UK

Copyright © 2012 by
University Press of America,® Inc.
4501 Forbes Boulevard
Suite 200
Lanham, Maryland 20706
UPA Acquisitions Department (301) 459-3366

10 Thornbury Road
Plymouth PL6 7PP
United Kingdom

All rights reserved

British Library Cataloging in Publication Information Available

Library of Congress Control Number: 2012936684
ISBN: 978-0-7618-5903-1 (paperback
eISBN: 978-0-7618-5904-8

Cover: Berliners rally in support of the Congress of
Workers Councils convened there on December 16th, 1918
(from Socialist Reproduction of London).

Dedicated to the memory of
Augustin Souchy and his comrades

Contents

Preface		vii
Chapter 1	Introduction	1
Chapter 2	Berlin	3
Chapter 3	The Urban Proletariat	7
Chapter 4	German Social Democracy	11
Chapter 5	The Trade Unions	21
Chapter 6	Wartime	31
Chapter 7	The Workers Councils	37
Chapter 8	Revolution	43
Chapter 9	1919	53
Chapter 10	1920	65
Chapter 11	Council Communism	69
Chapter 12	Conclusion	75

Appendices
A. Chronology 77
B. Abbreviations 81

Bibliography 83
About the Author 93

Preface

This study examines the rise, development and decline of revolutionary councils of industrial workers in Berlin following the collapse of the German empire at the end of the first World War. Apparently spontaneous in origin, these organizations of rank and file workers spread throughout Germany and included mutinous soldiers and sailors. This popular movement was without precedent in either the theory or practice of the Social Democratic party and the trade unions allied to it—the traditional organs of working class political expression in Imperial Germany.

The workers councils were most highly developed and organized in the capital city of Berlin, within its particular industrial, political and cultural milieu. The Berlin Shop Stewards group provided a hard core of militant revolutionaries within the movement, many of whose adherents were more moderate or ambiguous in their views. Externally, the councilists faced a hostile Social Democratic—trade union bureaucracy who characterized council rule as "wilde Sozialismus," a reconstituted and repressive state power, and a revolutionary rival in the rise of German Bolshevism. In the following pages the experience of the Berlin councils will be considered as alternative institutions outside of traditional union, party and governmental structures.

Chapter 1

Introduction

Back in the mid-1970s I had the pleasure and privilege of hosting Augustin Souchy as a house guest for several days. At that time Souchy was touring North America as the emissary of the revived Spanish National Confederation of Labor (Confederacion Nacional de Trabajo—CNT). This revolutionary syndicalist union was engaged in reconstituting itself following the death of General Franco, and was anxious to establish contact with foreign supporters. Souchy himself had been a life-long anarcho-syndicalist, a participant in the German Revolution and the Spanish Civil War, he once had argued with Lenin over revolutionary principles. Now in his eighties, Souchy had spent much of his later life traveling the world as an educator, journalist and researcher on the issues and problems of workers control and self-management (Souchy 1992).

Despite his age and the stress of traveling, neither of which seemed to affect his vitality, Souchy was quite forthcoming in taking the time to describe his various experiences and to present his thoughts on political and social topics. I became particularly interested in his discussion of the workers councils in Germany and their role as an alternative movement to both Social Democracy and Bolshevism.

Around this same period, I also had the opportunity of attending talks by Paul Mattick, another German who, like Souchy, had been active in revolutionary days in Berlin. Mattick had been a member of the anti-Bolshevik Communist Workers Party (Kommunistische Arbeiter-Partei Deutschlands—KAPD). In exile in America, he had made his living as a machinist, and had become a theoretician of council communism—a liberarian branch of Marxist thought.

The similarity in experiences and the conclusions drawn from them by these two veteran revolutionaries seemed to be of greater significance than any theoretical differences that might have separated them. In any case, since then I have maintained an abiding interest in the phenomenon of independent workers councils, particularly in the German context—one of the earliest attempts at achieving workers autonomy and control of production in the twentieth century. I hope that this paper will serve as a contribution to the study and understanding of this subject.

Chapter 2

Berlin

Regarded as one of the newer capitals of Europe, Berlin owes its modern facade largely to its rapid rate of growth in the late nineteenth century. Berlin's expansion in that period has been compared to that of North American cities like Chicago (Masur 1970: 132). But by the turn of the twentieth century, Berlin was at least the equal of her European counterparts not only in size, but in quality of urban life and cultural amenities. The metropolis had by then made the transition from what the German language defines as a great city—"Grosstadt," to that of a world-class city—"Weltstadt." With some two million inhabitants in 1900, Berlin would double in population within twenty years with the incorporation of its industrial suburbs into the municipality and expand in area to 90 square kilometers, the largest city in Europe after London (Watt 1968: 259; Gill 1993: 34). Given a national population of sixty million, approximately one of every fifteen Germans resided in Berlin or its immediate environs by the early years of the twentieth century (Peukert 1992: 7).

The center of the city was the site of spacious squares and parks, with affluent residential areas set off by massive government buildings and military headquarters (Diesel 1931: 101-102; *Berlin* 1985). Besides a large municipal bureaucracy, in its capacity as capital of the state of Prussia, Berlin also housed provincial administrative offices. But most notably, Berlin was the seat of government of the German Empire. This Greater Germany of Kaiser Wilhelm II stretched from the French border eastward to the frontiers of Russian Poland, from the Baltic south to the Alps, with colonies, spheres of influence, and commercial and strategic interests throughout Asia, Africa and the Western Hemisphere. The complex, sometimes overlapping jurisdictions of imperial, provincial and local administrations required a host of civil servants and public officials to staff the agencies and ministries of the various governmental units. Not least, imperial Berlin was the command center for the most powerful and efficient military establishment in Europe and the world. "In one sense," as a contemporary commentator noted, the city's "natural expression" was in large measure "the office and the barrack" (Diesel 1931: 100).

For Berlin, as for the German nation, the basis of imperial grandeur and military power lay in Germany's recent development from a mostly agrarian to an industrial, urbanized society. Like Chicago, Berlin was the center of a national transport system—by the twentieth century an extensive network of railways and canals (Diesel 1931: 52-54). The nationalized railroad system proved to be a motor of Berlin's accelerated industrial growth. Locomotive and freightcar repair shops and machine building enterprises became the basis for a giant metallurgical industry—from small workshops to large factory complexes. At the Berlin Industrial Exposition of 1879, engineers of the Siemens company demonstrated the first electric tramway and launched a new branch of industry. Siemens, along with the Allgemeine Elektrizitat Gesellschaft (AEG) made Berlin the center for the manufacture of electrical machines and components, resulting in the electrification of the entire German economy (Landes 1969: 287).

Expansion of the chemical industry was not far behind. From its origins in the mid-nineteenth century, utilizing coal by-products, production of chemicals boomed by 1900, aided by the extensive research and experimental facilities at the University of Berlin. The application of new electro-chemical processes and the discovery of synthetics stimulated growth in other branches of manufacture as well, in pharmaceuticals, optics, printing, and one of Berlin's oldest industries, textiles (Bruck 1962: 77; Masur 1970: 127-132).

As a late starter in heavy industrialization in comparison to Great Britain, German capital was in a position to take full advantage of the most advanced techniques in production and mechanical design. The models of Taylorism and Fordism, which shifted control of the labor process from the skilled workman to management, held a great interest for German industrialists. Berlin's Loewe machine tool plant, for example, erected in 1899, was able to immediately incorporate the latest

American manufacturing processes (Arnold 1985: 37; Landes 1969: 317). German commercial and technical organization allowed for the full integration of the various stages of production throughout heavy industry (Bruck 1962: 77).

While older factories and mills tended to be centrally located, Berlin's newer enterprises were found on the fringes of the city, spilling over into the working class suburbs. Metallurgical and electrical equipment concerns dominated north and east Berlin, with great arsenals and munitions works to the west (Watt 1968: 259). Entering the new century, in the words of a German historian, as "one branch of industry facilitated the expansion of others . . . all together formed an enormous network of industrial plants which extended from the center of Berlin to its farthest limits" (Masur 1970: 132).

Chapter 3

The Urban Proletariat

Prior to 1914, Berlin could be said to have been two cities—the one imperial, autocratic, tradition-bound—the other dynamic, turbulent, ultra-modern, with the power and majesty of the former dependent upon the vitality and energy of the latter. In one view, it was "the most practical and materialistic city in the world," yet with a "curious mixture of practicality and unreality" (Diesel 1931: 104). Some half of Berlin's citizens were dependent upon employment in industry, over 40% of them worked, or depended upon a breadwinner who worked, in the skilled or unskilled manual trades. Representing a majority in the greater Berlin area, industrial workers and their families were concentrated in the northern and eastern sections of the city, with large pockets near the city center. Working class neighborhoods like Neukoln or Wedding were characterized by long rows of crowded tenement apartment houses (Rosenhaft 1982: 174-175; Watt 1968: 255). During Berlin's years of economic expansion, housing for the working class was often constructed hastily—typically in apartment blocks surrounding narrow courtyards. Workers' flats were usually small, consisting of a kitchen and a bed-sitting room. Overcrowding was common, private lavatories a rarity (Gill 1993: 34). To a contemporary observer, the working class districts of Berlin were invariably,

> without form or character . . . Nothing helps to make more human the square blocks of stone of which these depressing neighborhoods are built. They have nothing warm or vital about them; the basis of everything is the trade union or the statistical report. . . . An atmosphere of sinister oppression and mechanical existence broods over them . . . (In

these) grey quarters . . . the 'comrades without a fatherland' led their miserable existence. (Diesel 1931: 102, 228)

While the metal-working and electro-technical industries were the chief employers, the construction trades followed close behind, offering a wide range of jobs from skilled carpenter to day laborer (McGuffie 1985: 208-209; Rosenhaft 1982: 174). From the turn of the century to the First World War, real weekly wages for workers rose only slightly, always somewhat below the steadily rising cost of living. (Miller and Potthoff 1983: 301-302). In the view of two historians of German Social Democracy, income for most workers,

> was only just sufficient for a moderately sized family to live on without serious food shortages but not to purchase adequate clothing as well and lead a life fit for human beings. In most working-class households it therefore remained literally vital that the wife should work as well. (Miller and Potthoff 1983: 43)

The working day averaged ten or more hours, with a 58-61 hour work week being the general norm (Schneider 1991: 397).

Because of the chronic need for trained operatives in Berlin's technical and capital-intensive enterprises, the municipality expended one-quarter of the city budget on elementary and secondary public education. The city further allowed free use of some of its classrooms to charitable organizations who tutored working class children after regular school hours, and often provided their charges with free dinners (Masur 1970: 143). Municipal subsidy also funded an extensive system of public libraries, and free or low-cost adult education programs.

For those young adolescents who did not attend the German equivalent of high school and instead went off to work, local government provided a second level of regular education—the trade continuation schools (Gewerbeschulen). Under the Imperial Trade Act of 1891, employers were legally required to allow all their workers under the age of eighteen, both male and female, to attend vocational schools during regular working time for a set number of hours per week—usually six—for a period of three years. Education was further supplemented by periods of apprenticeship training in industry. Nearly all skilled workers, at least through the turn of the century, received such Handwerk (artisanal) training, which imparted a shared sense of craft and control over the work environment. In the Berlin metallurgical works, apprenticeships typically lasted from three to four years (McGuffie 1985: 232-233, 246; Nolan 1986: 373). According to the economic historian David Landes, German industrial and technical education was superior to that of the rest of the industrialized world,

> (1) the ability to read, write, and calculate; (2) the working skills of the craftsman and mechanic; (3) the engineer's combination of scientific principle and applied training; and (4) high-level scientific knowledge, theoretical and applied. In all four areas, Germany represented the best that Europe had to offer; in all four, with the possible exception of the second, Britain fell far behind. (1969: 340)

And Berlin epitomized this educational system in Imperial Germany that had by the beginning of the twentieth century, "publically serviced the requirements of the large concerns and underwrote the basic class structure of the Reich" (McGuffie 1985: 253).

At the same time that technical and vocational training was being perfected in Berlin, a countervailing tendency was already underway in the city's manufacturing complexes. Foreign and domestic competition exerted pressure within enterprises toward the simplification of productive tasks and procedures and an increase in the pace and intensity of the work process—not excepting the skilled trades. In an 1906 study of the Berlin engineering industry, an economist was able to observe that,

> Right in Berlin there is still a whole series of small machine shops where . . . older, experienced workers . . . carry out the most varied operations, one after another, as they arise in production. In the modern engineering works, by contrast, casts or forgings wander from the bench of one worker to that of another after every single specialized task. A second worker now adds his labour and then passes the piece onto a third worker, who, for his part, knows nothing of the specialized production tasks of his predecessors. His competence does not extend one hairbreadth further than boring a hole of prescribed diameter into something with a machine at the exact spot designated to him . . . there was, and to a certain extent still is, a greater variety and diversity of separate production tasks in the older machine shops. So far, human labour has not yet become a mere appendage of the machine, which is the case in the machine shops of the large engineering works. . . .

> All this causes the position of the worker in the modern engineering works to be completely different from that in the older machine shops. The machine builder in the old, many sided sense has become extinct. The worker has become a specialist who only learns certain parts of a job, and this he does from scratch again and again. (McGuffie 1985: xxiii, xx)

In the 1880s Imperial Chancellor Bismarck had promulgated welfare legislation for workers, including sickness and accident insurance and old age pensions, making Germany the first nation to do so (Steinmetz 1991: 23-24). These benefits were provided, however, with a political purpose in mind. Social insurance guaranteed by the state, in the words of Kaiser Wilhelm I, was designed to "take the wind out of the sails of Social Democracy" (Steinmetz 1991: 29; Hamerow 1985: 29-30). Following upon Bismark's initiative, the city of Berlin and the Prussian state undertook the construction of municipal and state hospitals and clinics, the majority in working class districts. These institutions were considered to be superior in quality of care to their counterparts in the other great cities of Europe and America (Masur 1970: 142-143).

But however these measures were welcomed by the working class of Imperial Germany, it hardly dimmed their enthusiasm for the more egalitarian social order promised to them by the Social Democrats. In the view of some, it could hardly be otherwise,

> The Almighty Trinity, Army-Administration-Industry, set the tone of the age amid the applause and rejoicings of the bourgeoisie. . . . A stupendous bureaucratic organization had been built up for the express purpose of dealing with the dangers that seemed to threaten from the proletarian section of the people. With the aid of laws and regulations (which were claimed to be an example to the rest of the world of what things should be) and all the trappings of officialdom, it was laid down exactly what conditions entitled a man to seek relief from poverty and starvation. But this brought no feeling of release or salvation to the working masses; it only barred their prison gates more firmly. The real object of such measures was to prevent the increasing splendor of the Reich from suffering any check. (Diesel 1931: 228, 229)

Chapter 4

German Social Democracy

Imperial Germany was a society highly cognizant of social status and rank, even within a relatively cosmopolitan Berlin. The class and caste lines between the hereditary nobility, the middle classes and the proletariat were clearly drawn. This was nowhere more obvious than in German industry, where employers, and their managers and foremen, were known for their strict authoritarianism (Miller and Potthoff 1983: 44). Regarded by the established order with a mixture of fear, contempt and condescension, it is not suprising that most of the organized working class expressed itself politically through the Sozialdemokratische Partei Deutschlands, the Social Democratic Party.

German Social Democracy had its origins among skilled craftsmen and middleclass intellectuals in the mid-nineteenth century. Its growth by 1878 had so alarmed the established order that Chancellor Bismarck pushed an anti-socialist law through the Reichstag aimed at the repression of the nascent party and trade unions. Under its provisions, thousands of radicals and unionists were imprisoned, their meetings banned and publications proscribed (Schneider 1991: 51-52; Berger 1995: 72). While severely hampering socialist activities, the legislation at the same time did not forbid electoral participation and representation in the Imperial parliament and the provincial assemblies (perhaps because these institutions were possessed of only limited power). Between the promulgation of the Sozialistengesetz in 1878 and its repeal in 1890, socialist voting strength actually increased from 102,000 to 1,427,000, garnering some 20% of the popular vote and 35 seats in the Reichstag. In Berlin, five of the city's six electoral districts voted solidly Social Democratic from 1893 on, often in numbers far exceeding nominal party membership. By 1912 the SPD was able to poll four and one quarter million votes nationally, nearly 35% of the electorate, and become the largest party in the the Imperial parliament with 110 seats (Miller and Potthoff 1983: 34, 40-41, 294; Steenson 1981: 42; Gay 1962: 117). Party membership in that year reached over one million, making the SPD by far the largest political party in Germany, the Greater Berlin area accounting for some 13% of the national total (Steenson 1981: 94; Tegel 1987: 22). In the same period some 13,000 Socialists were elected to local and municipal offices, and another estimated 100,000 were members of local representative and administrative bodies dealing with sickness and accident insurance, pensions and industrial relations (Miller and Potthoff 1983: 48; Steinmetz 1991: 24-28, 30-31, 37-39). Socialist newspapers and periodicals circulated among millions of readers (Steenson 1981: 132-133). By the second decade of the twentieth century, the SPD had emerged as the first mass political party of the modern era. It was the flagship, the model organization of the Socialist International.

The typical party member, and socialist trade unionist, was an industrial worker, skilled or semi-skilled, male, Protestant and urban (Steenson 1981: 94-95; Miller and Potthoff 1983: 41). Residential housing patterns in Berlin and the other large cities of Germany broke down along class lines, with workers often living near their workplaces. Given that the "most compelling feature of the socialist, working-class movement in Imperial Germany was its isolation from and ostracism by the rest of society" (Steenson 1981: 111), it is hardly suprising that the segregation of working people within their own neighborhoods encouraged feelings of community and solidarity—all the more so as the proletarian was the object of official suspicion and scorn (Nolan 1986: 374). The local taverns and beer halls were usually the most convenient meeting places for Social Democrats, trade unionists and various workers' associations, as well as centers for informal socializing (Steenson 1981: 142-143; Lidtke 1985: 21; Roberts 1982: 82). The sheer size and vitality of the Social Democratic Party, and the concentration of its adherents in the urban areas, facilitated the development of a host of voluntary organizations and clubs—social, cultural, recreational and educational. These included gymnast and sports clubs, dramatic societies, chorales, musical performance groups, literary circles. Combined with party and trade union organization, this ubiquitous network constituted a vast Social Democratic subculture within Imperial Germany, an alternate culture (Lidtke 1985: 21-49). Membership in such associations,

> could quickly label a worker as a malcontent and a trouble maker. . . . Even the timid were gaining emancipatory experience by affiliating in some way with the labor movement. With that simple step they were defying the wishes of the kaiser and his ministers, rejecting the admonitions of clergymen and teachers, and bringing on themselves the hostile and often capricious supervision of the police and military. . . . To enroll in a club known to have labor movement connections . . . was tantamount to taking a political stand because it implied a set of preferences—political, ideological, social—that were unacceptable to most other segments of German society (Lidtke 1985: 16-17).

Indeed government officials even feared that these socialist organizations were becoming attractive to members of the middle classes (Lidtke 1985: 101).

Whether this Social Democratic associationalism in fact formed a separate culture within an autocratic state, or whether it was rather a means of the "negative integration" of the German working class into the larger society, has been the subject of considerable debate among historians of Imperial Germany (Roth 1963; Eley 1984: 15-20; Lidtke 1985: 3-20).

Within the city of Berlin, these workers clubs and and societies were popular and thriving institutions (Lidtke 1985: 22-23, 33, 34, 148). Berlin club members placed themselves in the forefront of resistance to the movement for centralization and Vereinsmeierei (amalgation) of the associations under the aegis of the SPD's Central Education Commission. The Berliners preferred to retain local control and the intimacy and camaraderie of relatively small organizations (Lidtke 1985: 72-74).

By the time of the Erfurt party conference of 1891, German Social Democracy, under the leadership of its leading theoretician Karl Kautsky, had clarified its ideology and specified its program. It based its principles and goals almost verbatim on the works of Karl Marx and Frederich Engels. The inevitable class struggle between worker and exploiter would culminate in the collapse of the capitalist system, the seizure of political power by the oppressed proletarian masses and the socialization of the means of production for the benefit of humanity. The state would wither away. This was affirmed to be the inexorable law of historical development. What was missing from this official declaration was reference to any specific means that would be employed to bring about the "inevitable" socialist revolution (Miller and Potthoff 1983: 38-40, 240-242; Mitchell and Stearns 1971: 81-83).

On the other hand, many of the immediate goals of Social Democracy proclaimed at Erfurt, such as constitutional reform, extension of the franchise, equality for women, secular and compulsory education, were quite compatible if not identical with the traditional platform of German liberal democrats since the failed Revolution of 1848 (Miller and Potthoff 1983: 47-48, 241-242; Hamerow 1972: 128-131). It was the legacy of repression of the Bismarck years that was in large part responsible for the gap between the socialist ideal and the business of practical politics. On the one hand, a residue of deep mistrust and hostility to the state remained among party and trade union rank and filers, and found expression in the revolutionary pronouncements of the SPD. But conversely, the fact that the anti-socialist laws had still permitted socialist electoral activities could not but encourage a reformist practice in a party struggling for its survival. So while party theory preached Marx's doctrine of revolution, everyday political methods remained within the realm of the practical, and after a time, tended toward the expedient (Miller and Potthoff 1983: 35-37).

Internally, the Party itself grew apace. With a membership of one million by 1914, organizational needs required the recruitment of a cadre of salaried officers and functionaries to replace the volunteers and part-time activists of an earlier era. Local and regional secretaries and administrators began to be appointed to their positions and paid by the national party office, and thus became responsible to the national executive (Schorske 1972: 128-129). By 1913 the SPD employed 4,000 full-time officials, with 750 of these assigned to Berlin (Mitchell and Stearns 1971: 97). The growth of a professional party administration and officialdom that has been described as a "self-serving, self-perpetuating, and conservatizing" force interposing "successive layers of national, state, and local bureaucracies" between the SPD leadership and the rank and file could only have a deadening effect upon inter-party debate and democratic procedures (Steenson 1981: 231, 232). Meanwhile the party apparatus expanded to encompass a host of subsidiary enterprises, including various cooperatives, building societies, inns, and some 62 printing works that employed over 10,000 workers (Mitchell and Stearns 1971: 97). Membership figures, dues payments and electoral statistics came to be the major preoccupation of the SPD. Organization became an end in itself, exemplified perhaps in the rise of Friedrich Ebert to the party's national secretariat. Ebert, colorless in personality and determined in effort, has been called the Stalin of Social Democracy for his talent at bureaucratic manipulation and singleminded efficiency, talents which would take him far. (Schorske 1972: 123-125). Such a development was unavoidable, according to the contemporary sociologist Robert Michels, the great observer and critic of the German Social Democratic Party,

> The technical specialization that inevitably results from all extensive organization renders necessary what is called expert leadership. Consequently the power of determination comes to be considered one of the specific attributes of leadership, and is gradually withdrawn from the masses to be concentrated in the hands of the leader alone. Thus the leaders . . . soon emancipate themselves from the mass and become independent of its control. . . . The mechanism of the organization . . . induces serious changes in the organized mass, completely inverting the respective position of the leaders and the led. As a result of organization, every party or . . . union becomes divided into a minority of directors and a majority of directed. (1962: 70)

Three factions had evolved within German socialism by the early years of the twentieth century. A right wing, represented by the revisionist Eduard Bernstein, argued that socialism could be attained gradually without the trauma of violent revolution, through electoral activity and parliamentary legislation. Bernstein and his adherents within the SPD held to this position even though the Reichstag at that time was able to exert only minimal influence upon national policy compared to the parliaments of Britain and France. Bernstein further urged the Social Democrats to formally renounce revolutionary Marxism and candidly admit that theirs was a party of radical democratic reform, the better to attract the support of other social strata outside the working class (Gay 1962: 146-151, 161-165, 220-237).

The traditional Marxist old guard, installed in the higher party offices and trade union bureaucracy, constituted the SPD center. Party theoreticians Karl Kautsky and August Bebel assured the party faithful that the eventual and inevitable collapse of the capitalist economy would bring down the old social order, and usher in the socialist commonwealth. This was ordained by the laws of historical development, and was merely a matter of time. Reformist tactics were theoretically acceptable within the context of this Marxian dialectic, since the party had to maintain its flexibility and in Bebel's phrase remain "armed for any eventuality" (Miller and Potthoff 1985: 50-51; Schorske 1972: 20). Kautsky rather ambiguously observed that the SPD was a "revolutionary, not a revolution-making party" that must follow a "strategy of attrition" until the final crisis of capitalist society (Steenson 1981: 207).

But the inability of the Social Democrats to translate electoral successes into real political influence increasingly frustrated and agitated the more radical forces within the party. In the 1890s, an opposition group calling itself Die Jungen (The Young Ones) challenged the orthodox leadership of the SPD with revolutionary manifestos and syndicalist-style rhetoric. The Berlin faction of the group formed a Union of Independent Socialists within the party. But their efforts were short-lived and made relatively little impact, and they succeeded in earning the opprobrium of Friedrich Engels himself (Rocker 1985: 10-13; Steenson 1981: 236; Bock 1969: 13). By this time the composition of national and regional congresses and committees of the SPD began to be weighted disproportionately away from the large urban areas like Berlin toward the smaller towns and more rural areas. This was done to encourage the expansion of the party in these regions where the organization was relatively weak. The immediate effect of this policy was to weaken radical influence and move the SPD in a more moderate direction (Schorske 1972: 129-135; Geary 1981: 119).

A more serious leftist opposition within the party took shape after 1900 around the question of the tactic of the general strike. General strikes were beginning to occur in other West European nations, usually over issues of suffrage reform (Schorske 1972: 33). An early advocate of such syndicalist tactics within the Social Democracy at this time was Dr. Raphael Friedeberg, a veteran party activist. In August of 1904, Friedeberg circulated a discussion paper at a conference of Berlin trade unionists entitled "Parliamentarianism and General Strike" in which he asserted that,

> The separation of the proletarian movement into political party and trade union, results in the neutralization of the unions, directs their attention almost exclusively to the terms of the labor contract, and has given the death blow to the idea of class struggle. (Bock 1969:28)

Even at best, Friedeberg insisted, parliamentarianism could do little to improve the situation of the great mass of workers. It was the daily struggle between capital and labor that produced the genuine socialist spirit in each individual worker. Each worker's personality would be liberated and develop positively as he participated in direct, mass action and the struggle for control of production and consumption—control for which each individual would be responsible. Parliamentarianism fatally enervated this vital and necessary process. Strikes, boycotts, May Day celebrations, demonstrations, all these experiences were prerequisite for the liberation of the proletariat, whose final triumph would take place with the General Strike. Syndicalist in all but name, Friedeberg and his fellow militants emphasized the subjective motivations and inspired activities of the individual worker in bringing about the social revolution, in obvious contrast to the historical determinism preached by the traditional Marxist leadership of the SPD (Bock 1969: 28-29; Schorske 1972: 35).

The events of the Russian Revolution of 1905 had a profound effect upon the left wing of German Social Democracy. The sudden and dramatic appearance of soviets, councils of industrial workers, occupying the factories and crowding the streets of St. Petersburg and Moscow in revolt against autocracy made the cautious electoralism of the SPD leadership appear relatively impotent and irrelevant. Leon Trotsky, prominent in the Petersburg soviet and later one of the great figures of the Bolshevik Revolution, described the origin of the factory councils as,

> A need born of the course of events. It was an organization which was authoritive and yet had no tradition; which could immediately invoke a scattered mass of hundreds of thousands of people while having virtually no organizational machinery; which united the revolutionary currents within the proletariat; which was capable of initiative and spontaneous self-control—and most important of all could be brought out from underground within twenty-four hours (1971: 104).

Among others within the radical wing of the Social Democratic Party, the activist and theoretician Rosa Luxemburg drew very definite conclusions from the Russian events. She had studied the outbreak of the general strikes in Western Europe, commenting in 1902 that a "general strike forged *in advance* within the fetters of legality is like a war demonstration with cannons whose charge has been dumped into a river within the very sight of the enemy" [emphasis in original] (Froelich 1972: 129). This, she shortly discovered, was not at all the case in Russia.

At pains to disassociate herself from the anarcho-syndicalists and anarchists who preached the general strike, Luxemburg termed the Russian variant the "mass strike" (Bock 1969: 30). In her comparison and analysis of the workers movements in Tsarist Russia and Imperial Germany, "The Mass Strike, the Political Party and the Trade Unions," she noted that the 1905 Revolution was the first historical experiment on a very large scale with this means of struggle. The mass strike "is not artificially 'made' . . . not propagated . . . but . . . results from social conditions. . . . (It) is . . . *the method of motion of the proletarian mass*, the phenomenal form of the proletarian struggle in the revolution" [emphasis in original] (Luxemburg 1971: 9, 16, 45). The mass strike was a new method of revolutionary struggle—the product of the industrial and technological development of the new century, and of new social and political realities that had to be recognized by a conscious and renovated socialist movement. Although the Social Democrats might be the vanguard of the workers movement, it was still impossible to consider that the proletarian revolution could be the work of a mere well-organized minority:

> Every real, great class struggle must rest upon the support and cooperation of the widest masses, and a strategy of class struggle . . . based upon the idea of the finely stage-managed march out of the small well-trained part of the proletariat is foredoomed to be a miserable fiasco. Mass strikes . . . depend not so much upon 'discipline' and 'training' . . . as upon a real revolutionary, determined class action, which will be able to win and draw into the struggle the widest order of the unorganized workers. . . . In the case of the enlightened German worker the class consciousness implanted by the Social Democrats is *theoretical and latent*. . . . A year of revolution has . . . given the Russian proletariat that 'training' which thirty years of Parliamentary and trade union struggle cannot artificially give to the German proletariat [emphasis in original]. (Luxemburg 1971: 66, 67)

The concept of the Mass Strike and allied tactics as advanced by Rosa Luxemburg ignited heated debate within the ranks of the SPD and the trade unions. Proceeding from Luxemburg's emphasis upon the relative spontaneity of mass action, the party militant Anton Pannekoek attacked Kautsky and the party old guard for what he considered to be their mechanical conception of organization and class struggle. In his 1912 essay "Marxist Theory and Revolutionary Tactics," Pannekoek insisted that

> the spirit of organization is in fact the active principle which alone endows the framework of organization with life and energy. . . . The spirit is not something abstract or imaginary by contrast with the 'concrete' organization, but is just *as concrete and real* as the latter. . . . If organizations are able to develop and take action as powerful, stable, united bodies, if . . . neither struggle nor defeat can crack their solidarity . . . they do not do so because of the . . . statutes, nor because of the magic power of the organization's funds or its democratic constitution: the reason for all this lies in the proletarian sense of organization, the profound transformation that its character has undergone [emphasis in original]. (Pannekoek and Gorter 1978:57-58)

Rosa Luxemburg and the Social Democratic left wing were convinced that the class conscious instincts and innate capabilities of the masses had been demonstrated once and for all during the course of the Russian Revolution. But the Russian events, and the polemics of the radicals, had seemingly little effect upon the officials of the SPD. "General Streik ist General Unsinn!" (The general strike is general nonsense!) was a common expression among more conservative party members. Even apart from the fear that such insurrectionary tactics would endanger party and union treasuries, property holdings and governmental sinecures, many party professionals regarded their own constituents with a certain mixture of paternalism and mild contempt. The increasing distance between the party leadership and the rank and file did nothing to persuade most SPD theoreticians and bureaucrats that workers might possibly have developed their own conceptions of democracy and solidarity from their experiences at the workplace and in the community, and might have made an interpretation of socialist ideology immediately relevant to their daily lives.

Indeed, many Social Democrats had little understanding of behavior that was unlawful or not "respectable." They combined a rejection of such practices as heavy drinking or industrial sabotage with the fear that the working class of Imperial Germany would be distracted or corrupted by the burgerliche (bourgeois) culture that surrounded them—the same bourgeois culture that so many of the party elite themselves had presumably absorbed in the universities and professions (Lidtke 1985: 196-198;

Geary 1987: 15-16; Roberts 1982). The Party's Berlin daily *Vorwaerts* expressed a rather smug confidence that the cultural level of the downtrodden could be elevated under the proper tutelage:

> The Party can count on the fact that its moral influence on the proletariat is stronger than the bad customs of the past and the tremendous force of habit. Social Democracy can count on this fact because its educational work in the working class has gone on for decades. (Roberts 1982: 90)

As for the nearly 90% of the German work force that was unorganized, the great mass whose active participation Luxemburg and the radicals considered indispensible for the victory of social revolution, a significant portion was evidently regarded with distrust and disdain by many in the Social Democracy. One SPD veteran contrasted the skilled craftsman with the unskilled laborer in pointed language:

> On the one side there is the cultivated and refined portion of the working class, seeking the highest treasures of humanity and equality with the ruling classes; and on the other, the Lumpenproletariat, depraved through Schnapps, ignorance, misery and want, the dregs of human society, which knows only base, animal instincts and wastes away without the least spiritual or intellectual involvement. (Roberts 1982:110)

As noted above, in industries like metal-working, the early years of the century saw the introduction of semi-skilled and unskilled workers into previously skilled workplaces. For some in the skilled ranks, their new workmates often seemed crude and aggressive, with no interest in politics or in the processes of production itself, poor material for the SPD to work with (Roth 1977: 37).

Evidently, there was a general opinion among German Social Democrats, in fact if not in theory, that the inevitable breakdown of capitalist society (at some indefinite time in the future) would elevate them to power more or less non-violently, and permit them to direct, educate and guide the majority of their less enlightened constituents into the promised land of socialism.

Chapter 5

The Trade Unions

The growth in the ranks of socialist labor was even more spectacular than that of the SPD itself—from over 290,000 members of the Allgemeiner Deutscher Gewerkschaftbund (Free Trade Unions) in 1890 to more than two and one half million by 1913 (the figures for the Catholic and Liberal union federations for that year were over 300,000 and some 100,000 members respectively). These figures accounted for about 12% of Germany's non-agricultural work force. (The percentage of unionized workers in the United States at this time was 8.5%.) The city of Berlin itself was a union stronghold with 5.6% of the national workforce and nearly ten percent of Germany's trade union membership (Schneider 1991: 384; Steenson 1981: 94-95). This great increase took place alongside a rapidly expanding national economy. The number of workers in industry doubled between 1887 and 1914, as labor productivity kept equal pace (Miller and Potthoff 1983: 42). Labor organization usually followed traditional craft lines with the exceptions of industrial-type unions in enterprises like metal working and construction (Schneider 1991: 74). Union membership grew steadily despite a particularly hostile social environment. Besides the general prohibition against union membership and the right to strike, employers "consciously increased the divisions amongst the working class by creating a system of benefits and rewards for some workers, whilst simultaneously introducing a rigorous factory discipline for all" (Berger 1995: 71). Wage differentials were significant: the average annual wage for printers in 1907 was 1,317 marks, while a textile worker averaged 594 marks for the year. In the textile industry itself, a skilled male worker earned 44.1 pfennigs per hour, and a skilled female only 30.7 (Berger 1995: 73).

Class conflict did not slacken throughout this period. The lockout was used increasingly by employers after 1900, and in the years from 1899 through 1913 an annual average of over 2,100 strikes took place in Germany—mainly over wages and length of the working day—with the number of strikers (including those locked out) averaging over 250,000 per year (Schorske 1972: 180; Schneider 1991: 389; Geary 1981: 101). Clearly, trade union growth was largely dependent upon the "tremendous importance of industrial struggle as a driving force" (Schneider 1991: 97).

By 1900 the Free Trade Unions alignment with Social Democracy began to undergo a change. The unions no longer regarded themselves as mere auxillaries to the socialist movement, or recruiting agents for the SPD. They asserted their independence from the party within the context of a working relationship, each entity defined as a necesssary "pillar" of the movement at large (Schorske 1972: 15-16; Schneider 1991: 89-90). Measuring success by numbers of workers organized, the unions generally saw themselves as non-political in their efforts to attract the disparate elements of the unorganized workforce. Of necessity they concerned themselves with the immediate problems of wage rates, working conditions and the revision of restrictive laws, speculations about the future socialist commonwealth took second place. Throughout the 1890s the trade unions managed to construct an impressive system of social benefits for their members, part of the Social Democrats' "alternative society," featuring sickness and death benefits, compensation schemes and strike funds (Schneider 1991: 74, 103-104, 72).

But with organizing successes came a growing conservatism within the higher echelons of the union leadership. Indeed, as early as 1889, Carl Legien, the chairman of the General Commission of the ADGB, had no hesitation in demonstrating his slight regard for the tenets of Marxist theory. Speaking before a union congress in that year he insisted that the "organized workers do not want the so-called crash to come, forcing us to create institutions on the ruins of society, regardless of whether they are better or worse than the present ones. We want peaceful development" (Schneider 1991: 89). The fact that the Anti-Socialist Law was still on the books at that time may have influenced Legien's remarks, but the policies he pursued in the following decades seem to confirm his early sentiments. In any case by 1906 the Free Trade Unions and the SPD formalized the former's independence and influence within the socialist movement with the Mannheim Agreement that henceforth required the party to consult with the unions before embarking on any major policy initiatives. The Mannheim talks between party and union leadership had been originally initiated to deal with the general strike question—an issue which had so agitated the SPD, and to which the General Commission was emphatically opposed. It was officially agreed that the general strike was a tactic to be applied only as a defensive measure, i.e. to defend the franchise (Berger 1995: 72-73; Schneider 90-92). The discussions between party and union leaders leading up to the Mannheim Agreement and the suppression of the general strike tactic had been clandestine, until a group of radical trade unionists in Berlin secured the records and published an account they called "A Look Behind the Scenes" (Bock 1969: 26). Rosa Luxemburg and the socialist left rejected the Mannheim accord. Such an agreement revealed that "the influence and power of the trade unions are founded upon the upside down theory of the incapacity of the masses for criticism and decision" (Luxemburg 1971: 87). This attitude was the result of the development of a trade union officialdom which inclined itself to,

> The specialization of professional activity . . . bureaucraticism and a certain narrowness of outlook. . . . the overvaluation of the organization, which from a means has gradually been changed into an end in itself, a precious thing, to which the interests of the struggles should be subordinated. . . . In close connection with these theoretical tendencies is a revolution in the relations of leaders and rank and file. In place of the direction by colleagues through local committees, with their admitted inadequacy, there appears the business direction of the trade union officials. The initiative and the power of making decisions thereby devolve upon trade union specialists . . . and the more passive virtue of discipline upon the mass of members. (Luxemburg 1971: 87, 88)

The expansion of the trade union bureaucracy and administration had paralleled that of the SPD. While in 1900 there were 269 union officials and employees, there were nearly 3,000 by 1914 (Schneider 1991: 75; Steenson 1981: 96). Along with organizational growth came a strong trend toward the centralization of authority and decision-making. As a historian of German labor has noted: "In the eyes of the General Commission trade union policy was principally organizational policy" (Schneider 1991: 72). This policy was justified by the trade union center by the necessity to marshall and rationalize resources and finances in the battle with the powerful employers associations.

But the creation of a union hierarchy had formalized and depersonalized the relations between rank and file and union officer, perhaps similiar to that existing between worker and employer in the factory (Domansky 1989: 337). Indeed, in 1912 the *Neue Zeit* (New Times), theoretical organ of the socialist party, rather frankly (and somewhat condescendingly) described the contradictory state of affairs within the unions:

> Trade union struggle places ever greater demands on the discipline of its members. The conditions of trade-union life have become more complicated, because the struggles are no longer so easy to conduct as formerly. Particularly in times of crisis, the workman in the shop becomes pessimistic concerning his organization. . . . The fundamental atmosphere in broad sectors of the trade union membership is a kind of syndicalist undercurrent . . . an atmosphere of despair: the union is not successful enough for the men in the shop, the tactic too cautious, the leaders too circumspect, and since cause and effect are not always clear to him, he is readily inclined in meetings to let himself be whipped up into opposition to the leaders. (Schorske 1972: 261)

Those who constituted the "syndicalist undercurrent" and coalesced around a radical opposition to the union leadership were the so-called "localists" within the German trade union movement. The localists set themselves at odds with the General Commission and the trade union leadership over basic questions of organization, tactics and ideology. They were particularly strong in the Berlin area and within industrial-type unions like construction and the metal working trades. Beginning in the 1890s, the localists consistently resisted centralization of union power and authority, and attempted to retain their own autonomy. Adverse to bureaucracy and the negotiation of formal contracts, they advocated the unity of economic and political struggle and engagement in direct action (Bock 1969: 26; Schneider 1991: 73).

Localist union branches of national organizations were at first able to exercise a substantial degree of control of trade union activities in municipalities like Berlin through the formation of "cartels" (roughly corresponding to American city-wide trade union councils) and control of local strike funds. Until this control was eventually undermined by the General Commission, the cartels could assume a combatative stance toward local employers and have wide latitude in determining their own course of action (Schorske 1972: 9-10).

In 1897, some localist dissidents formed their own union, based on the Berlin construction trades, the Free Association of German Trade Unions (Freie Vereingung deutscher Gewerkschaften), with the bricklayer Fritz Kater elected as chairman (Rocker 1985: 14). As a veteran militant and radical, Kater was a popular choice. In a previous meeting of the Berlin bricklayers' shop commission, Kater had made his views clear: "The battle cannot be successfully waged through the passage of legislation. . . . class struggle requires the use of the general strike, direct action, sabotage, (so-called) passive resistance . . . carried out on economic terrain" (Bock 1969: 32). But the FVdG was prevented from offering a clear-cut alternative to the Free Trade Unions by the lingering connection of many of its rank and file to the mainstream socialist movement. Finally in 1908 the Social Democratic Party expelled its members within the independent union for their adherence to anti-electoralism and the dogma of the general strike. (Rocker 1985: 16; Schneider 1991: 73-74; Bock 1990: 60-62). The FVdG had a fluctuating membership, from a high of some 20,000 in 1901 to around 6,000 at the beginning of the World War (Freie Arbeiter Union 1986: 5; Bock 1990: 61).

The conflict between centralism and localism, business unionism and syndicalism, determinism and subjectivity was perhaps nowhere more marked than within the ranks of the German Metal Workers Union (Deutscher Metallarbeiter-Verband). Founded in 1891, the DMV was the first labor union in Germany to organize itself along industrial lines. Its growth following the turn of the century was rapid, and by 1911 it was Germany's largest labor organization consisting of more than half a million members, with close to 20% of all metal workers within its ranks (Domansky 1989: 321, 324;

Schneider 1991: 74). The union leadership followed the orthodox Marxist line of the Erfurt Program in theory, and the policies of the General Commission in practice. They believed that the concentration and centralization of capital in Imperial Germany required formation of industrial unions to counter the massed resources of the employers associations (Domansky 1989: 324). But despite its size, the DMV faced a major problem in the years before the First World War. The union's strength lay in medium-sized and smaller enterprises. It was generally unable to make significant inroads into the sector of heavy industry, such as steelworks, which employed a higher percentage of semi-skilled and unskilled workers than did smaller factories. By 1913, 75% of the union membership remained skilled workers—turners, moulders, shipwrights, and the like (Domansky 1989: 326, 342). Aside from the ability of larger firms to resist unionization, the officials of the DMV were to a great extent hampered by their own ideological assumptions. They took quite seriously the mechanistic theory of social evolution propounded by Kautsky and the other members of the old guard of the SPD. According to them, socialism could only emerge following the full and complete development of the capitalist forces of production. Rejection or resistance to the new rationalized forms of the productive process was hopelessly reactionary and held up progress toward socialism. For example, the DMV was willing to give up its opposition to Sunday and overtime work because it did not want to obstruct labor processes that might incorporate the advanced state of technology. The introduction of scientific management became ubiquitous, particularly applicable in the sector of heavy industry, but also affecting the more traditional artisanal production systems in smaller workplaces and thereby provoking the workforce. Some metal workers complained of nervous exhaustion in the factory, and engaged in "striking on the job"—intentionally lowering productivity (Domansky 1989: 327-329, 337, 391-392; Geary 1981: 123). Thus for many workers,

> the DMV was a union that oriented its action less on the concrete interests of workers than on theoretical assumptions about the development of the forces of production. . . . A parodoxical situation emerged in which the industrial union, as conceived by the DMV, did not address the needs of the modern industrial workers. (Domansky 1989: 328, 329)

While awaiting the transformation from capitalism to socialism which technological development would make inevitable, the Metal Workers directorate adhered to the line of the General Commission—"quiet work in the usual way." The development of German trade unionism, Karl Kautsky reminded a union congress, was the result of decades of arduous, routine tasks. To the uproar over the general strike and class warfare, he assured the delegates that "We prefer calm" (Opel 1980: 23).

Besides the rejection of the revolutionary general strike, in theory or in practice, and the aversion even to May Day marches and demonstrations, the DMV hierarchy took a dim view of strikes of any sort. Social change would come about through historical processes, not by ill-considered strikes which could not really achieve any lasting gains for workers under an exploitive capitalist system. If strikes had to be conducted at all, they must be carefully staged and planned with order and discipline in mind. Raw emotion was to be avoided at all costs. Strikes of union locals could only take place with the approval of the DMV's governing board—defensive strikes had to be reported twentyfour hours in advance, offensive strikes required three months notification, and could only be carried out if extensive negotiation with the employer had failed. A local's demands had to be reasonable, as certified by the next highest organ of the union, the district administration of the DMV (Domansky 1989: 331-334). However these measures could not prevent the outbreak of unofficial strikes and wildcats wherever locals felt that they could defy their union leaders as well as their employers (Domansky 1989: 345-347: Opel 1980: 32-33).

The concentration of power at the executive level of the union made it increasingly hostile to any sort of criticism. Those comprising the leadership considered themselves professionals compared to the unsophisticated and emotional rank and file. At a union congress in 1907, a DMV official asserted that tactical decisions "in every single case" could only be determined within the "small councils of the administration . . . (by) a few representatives competent for their experience in such matters" (Opel 1980: 31,32).

The well-organized and independent metal workers of Berlin maintained their own organization until joining with the DMV in 1897. Their entry into the national body was only agreed to after they were promised complete autonomy on the strike question, even though this exception was contrary to the principles of the union. The adherence of the Berlin group greatly strengthened the existing localist and radical sentiment in the union, as well as provoking resentment on the part of other locals who did not possess their degree of autonomy. Eventually a union congress would cite the independence of the Berlin local as a "danger to the general welfare" (Domansky 1989: 325, 334).

The Berlin metal workers joined the other dissidents within the DMV in forming a significant opposition. The leadership was charged with "dictatorship" and "absolutism," to which the central board responded by accusing their critics of anarcho-syndicalism—a charge which was largely true, but which did nothing to deter or discredit the militants (Domansky 1989: 347-348). Confronted with Taylorism in the workshops and the increased use of the lockout by employers united in powerful federations, the DMV turned to lobbying the Reichstag to improve the working and living conditions of the industrial proletariat through remedial legislation, in concert with the practice of the General Commission of the Free Trade Unions and the hierarchy of the SPD (Domansky 1989: 348).

The radical left in Berlin, both inside and outside the traditional Social Democratic Party and trade unions, was able to function within a thriving political culture. The capital was the national center of politics, commerce and the arts, with a liberal middle class and a sophisticated urban proletariat. Headquarters of the SPD and its allied unions, here resided the leading figures of the various factions of the German socialist movement—Bernstein, Kautsky, Luxemburg, Ebert, Legien. For the militant workers and radical intellectuals of "Red" Berlin, anarcho-syndicalists, anarchists and revolutionary Marxists, the tension between the theoretical and formal adherence of the SPD to class struggle and its organizational conservatism was a constant incitement to action. These elements had been encouraged by the adoption of the Charter of Amiens by the French Confederation General du Travail (General Confederation of Labor) in 1906. This was a specifically anti-parliamentary syndicalist manifesto endorsing the general strike and assigning to the trade union the task of fomenting social revolution (Bock 1969: 26, 27-28, 30-31; Lorwin 1954: 312-313). There also evidence that returning emigres from America spread the doctrines of the Industrial Workers of the World throughout the German revolutionary left (Bock 1969: 124-126; Arnold 1985: 161).

Besides the publications, pamphlets and manifestos issuing from the radical wing of the SPD, there were a number of ultra-left periodicals and newsletters produced in Berlin aimed at a working class readership. Already in the 1890s, oppositionists in the socialist party had collaborated with anarchists to produce *Sozialist* (Socialist), while independent revolutionaries issued *Arbeiter- Zeitung* (Workers' Times) (Bock 1969: 14). Somewhat later the FVdG published *Die Einigkeit* (Unity) and *Die Pionier* (The Engineer) with a circulation of at least several thousand. The editor of the latter journal, Fritz Koester, likened the leaders of the Social Democratic Party to priests who encouraged the masses of working people to have faith in secular supersition—like the primacy of the law—and thereby stifle their revolutionary instincts (Bock 1990: 60; Bock 1969: 33). The Berlin ultra-left group Lichtstrahlen (Lightrays) produced the review *Arbeiterpolitik* (Workers Politics) from 1913 until its suppression in the early years of the war. Advertising itself as an organ for the "thinking worker," it accused the SPD of organizing itself according to the Imperial Prussian model. The real aim of the parliamentary socialists was the total control of the working people by the party and trade union bureaucracy (Bock 1969: 72-73). *Arbeiterpolitik*'s editor, Julian Borchardt, asserted that,

> We are convinced that the continuing development of the socialist masses will be destroyed by any blind faith in authority, upon which the military depends . . . (and) . . . will disappear like chaff in the wind, when all men possess the necessary degree of political education. And with that will also disappear the possibility that the masses blindly follow any leaders (Bock 1969: 73).

Arbeiterpolitik had most of its sales in Teltow and Charlottenburg and other working class districts of the city (Bock 1969: 73).

Beset by increasing internal tensions and contradictions since the turn of the century, the cohesion of the German socialist movement finally cracked under the pressure of the World War. Both within the Social Democracy, and the German Imperium itself, the gulf between hierarchy and rank and file, between official policy and everyday life in the trenches and on the factory floor, finally forced a breakdown of the traditional mechanisms of social organization and authority. Revolutionary elements would come to the fore, at least for a time, to lead the popular masses demanding an end to the war and the creation of a new and democratic social order.

Chapter 6

Wartime

Like their colleagues in the Second International, the French socialists and British laborites, the German Social Democrats voted for war credits in August 1914. Aside from the genuine nationalism that many within the party had always felt and expressed, and the passions aroused by a war against reactionary Tsarist Russia, the SPD leadership was fearful that opposition to the war would alienate them from the patriotic masses. With a good deal more justification, they were certain that any resistance would subject them to suppression and prosecution by the state, with the seizure of party property and the 20 million marks in the SPD treasury (Miller and Potthoff 1983: 55-57; Carsten 1982: 11-17; Schorske 1972: 285-291).

But the Social Democratic Party was willing to go further. Avoiding the role of even a loyal opposition, the party joined with the trade unions in adherence to the Burgfrieden, the Civil Peace, together with the employers associations and the government—a domestic truce for the duration of the war. Although nothing specific was promised by the Imperial authorities, the trade union and party officials expected that their loyalty would be rewarded by eventual recognition of their political legitimacy by the establishment. Party reformists in particular looked forward to the bestowing upon the SPD of Equal Rights, or Gleichberechtigung (Miller and Potthoff 1983: 57-58); Schorske 1972: 290-291; Schneider 1991: 111).

Within several weeks, Rosa Luxemburg, the Reichstag deputy Karl Liebknecht, and other leftists within the SPD began to draw together an opposition to party war policy. In the Berlin area, there was a sizeable segment of SPD activists willing to organize against the Burgfrieden. Luxemburg and her radical colleagues encouraged a constant round of meetings and provocative discussions in private homes and educational associations, the number and frequency of which frustrated the police (Carsten 1982: 15; Frolich 1972: 207). Karl Liebknecht soon broke party discipline and voted against war credits, becoming increasingly outspoken in his anti-militarist and social revolutionary pronouncements, both within parliament and in public. He quickly became the symbol of the left opposition (Trotnow 1984: 149-177). Other Reichstag dissidents of the SPD were emboldened to do the same (Miller and Potthoff 1983: 58).

The socialist party formally split at the beginning of 1917 with the expulsion by the majority of the leftist caucus within the SPD; shortly thereafter the latter militants formed the Independent (Unabhaengige) Social Democratic Party of Germany (USPD). This grouping was based upon the radical left but included pacifist revisionists like Eduard Bernstein. Opposition to the continuation of the war provided what cohesion there was. In the ensuing months, many in the USPD became close to the autonomous workers' movement alive in the workshops and factories of Berlin (Miller and Potthoff 1983: 58-60; Morgan 1975: 50-63).

The Free Trade Unions entered into the Burgfrieden with even less hesitation than the SPD itself. And this despite the fact, as at least one historian of the period has alleged, that "enthusiasm for the war among the working class does not seem to have been particularly great" (Bieber 1987: 75). Nevertheless, the General Commission expressed its full support for the Imperial war aims. They believed that victory would provide great economic advantages for the Reich in which the working class would share (Schneider 1991: 112). Further, they maintained a great faith in the potential of the Imperial state. Legien endorsed what he called "war socialism," the increasing control of the national economy by governmental decree. He was certain that state intervention in economic life was the first step toward a socialist society, one which would be introduced gradually by administrative fiat (Moses 1982: 200-201, 205-208).

With the passage of the Auxiliary War Service Act of 1916, the union finally achieved their long sought goal of legal recognition. Besides legitimizing their status, the Act provided for committees in each workplace to consult with management over wages and working conditions. Unions were given parity with employers on labor arbitration boards, presided over by army officers. The union leadership was thereby drawn into close cooperation with the state authorities and the military. For the rank and file, however, the Act had an even more direct impact upon their lives. All German males between the ages of 17 and 60 were subject to compulsory labor service if not already in uniform. Freedom of movement from job to job was abolished, with appeal subject to a mediation committee. The Auxilliary Service Act militarized the German labor force, a move which had been demanded at the beginning of the war by such as Ernst von Borsig, chairman of the Association of Berlin Engineering Manufacturers (Schneider 1991: 115-116, 118-119; Moses 1982: 204-205).

However pleased the trade union leadership may have been upon being granted admittance to the "national community," for the working classes of Germany the years 1914-1918 brought only misery. Though unemployment remained below 3% for most of the war and nominal wages rose, the soaring rate of inflation reduced purchasing power to below pre-war levels. By the middle of 1916, inflation had reached 100%. The real wages of male war industry workers fell by over 20%, while those in civilian industries suffered a real wage loss of more than 40% (Schneider 1991: 113; Ulrich 1987: 57-58; Carsten 1982: 74). Compounding this hardship was the increasing scarcity of foodstuffs. Conscription and the diversion of resources and materiel to the front resulted in the steady decline of agricultural production. Only some 60% as much wheat and potatoes were being harvested by 1918 compared to the last year before the war. In 1915 bread rationing was introduced, soon followed by meat, fat and milk. Food supplies not only became harder to obtain, but they deteriorated in quality and substitute foodstuffs made their appearance (Schneider 1991:120; Institut fur Marxismus-Leninismus 1968: 21; Ulrich 1987: 57). Soon meat, butter and eggs became luxury items, available only on the black market for the privileged who could afford the inflated prices. This was a source of bitter resentment on the part of industrial workers and the lower middle classes. The situation was worsened by the apparent incompetence of the civil authorities to efficiently transport and distribute what food supplies there were, a particular problem in Berlin (Ulrich 1987: 57; Masur 1970: 272: Winter 1993: 116-117).

Most Berliners apparently subsisted on around a thousand calories per day, and public health suffered accordingly. Supplies of coal were equally affected. The worst period of the entire war may have been the so-called "turnip winter" of 1916-17, when the stocks of both foodstuffs and heating materials were at their lowest point and the temperature in the city fell to -22 degrees Celsius (Pelz 1987: 88-90; Gill 1993: 6; Masur 1970: 274). To maintain production levels and reduce discontent among their employees, armaments firms and war industries resorted to the provision of factory canteens and supplemental food allowances—factors which did nothing to reduce disaffection and militancy in the workshops, and may even have encouraged it (Ulrich 1987: 58).

The first mass protests in wartime Berlin began in 1915 over rationing and food supplies and were usually led by women. But sentiment soon began to turn against the war itself. A petition to the SPD executive endorsed by over 700 local party functionaries demanded a peace initiative and the abrogation of the Burgfrieden—40% of the signatories were from Berlin. A meeting of district Social Democrats from around the city issued a call for "bread, freedom and peace," and the replacement of the party officialdom (Carsten 1982: 42-43, 44, 81-82; Ullrich 1987: 60-61). Anti-war sentiment was even encouraged and spread by soldiers on leave from the trenches (Carsten 1982: 78-79; Masur 1970: 280). On Mayday 1916, Karl Liebknecht and other members of the revolutionary Spartacist League organized an anti-war rally at the Potsdamer Platz in Berlin, attracting several thousand people (Trotnow 1984: 173). In his leaflet, Liebknecht called the Civil Peace a "betrayal of socialism." "Only a return to the gospel of socialism," he insisted, "to proletarian internationalism, can save the peoples, civilization, the workers' cause from the abyss" (Trotnow 1984: 173). Liebknecht and others of the left opposition were arrested while the demonstrators shouted "Peace" and "Long Live the International" until dispersed by the police (Trotnow 1984: 173, 176-177, Carsten 1982: 82-83). But by now an organized, grass-roots radical opposition was taking shape in the strategic war industries of Greater Berlin.

The enthusiasm with which the Free Trade Union officials greeted the Civil Peace and the Auxillary War Service Act completely severed whatever connection might have remained between union hierarchy and factory floor. Conscription and disaffection reduced union membership by one and one half million by 1916. In the place of those called to the colors, came thousands and thousands of women and youths, unskilled and lacking any experience of traditional trade unionism (Schneider 1991: 113-14; Arnold 1985: 37). The absence of any connection to a particular skill or occupation, and the difficulties of sudden adaptation to the discipline of the assembly line, heightened the sensitivity of these new operatives to their working environment—an environment that had become harsher under the pressure of war production. With longer hours and an intensified work pace, the rate of industrial accidents in German factories rose by 50% after 1914 (Schneider 1991: 119; Geary 1981: 137). The radical socialist Karl Retzlaw described the grim conditions in a Berlin munitions plant:

> The working conditions were like they must have been under early capitalism. There was always 'something wrong'. Especially during the night shift. Never a night passed without one or more of the women collapsing at their machines from exhaustion, hunger, illness. . . . On many days in winter there was no heating, the workers stood around in groups, they could not and would not work. . . . In the canteen there were almost daily screaming fits by women . . . because they claimed 'the ladle had not been filled.' (Ullrich 1987: 59)

The conscription of many shop stewards, the self-imposed limits on organizational activity coincident with the Civil Peace, the militarization of labor under the Auxiliary Service Act—all these factors had by 1916 practically divorced the trade unions from their basic functions in the factories and workshops. Legally, only the workers committees permitted by the Auxiliary Service law had the right to articulate the interests of the employees—a situation which some radical elements in the workshops were able to turn to their advantage. The trade union officials called upon the workers to be patient until the end of the war, to "hold out" until final victory (Schneider 1991: 113-114, 119, 126; Ullrich 1987: 78).

Now that the formal connection to the union executive bodies were for all practical purposes broken off, and recognized representation of workers' concerns limited to the committees, the localist factions within the Greater Berlin unions reverted to type. With their history of militancy and disdain for official authority and formality, they were well placed to become the channel of wartime discontent. Largely exempt from the military draft (except for certain ratings in the Imperial Navy), vital to the war effort, class conscious, well-schooled in political and organizational struggles, the skilled proletariat of industrial Berlin was possessed of wide experience and great self-confidence—individually and collectively. The wartime erosion of traditional occupational distinctions and the great influx of unskilled workers—often young and female—did nothing to limit their independence or diminish their radical energy. Indeed the merger of these apparently disparate groups of workers during a period of war and hardship created a mass revolutionary movement (Bock 1969: 81-82; Horn 1969: 11; Ullrich 1987: 59-60).

Chapter 7

The Workers Councils

The origins of the German workers council movement are to be found in the clandestine election of shop stewards (Obleute) in the metal works and munitions plants of Greater Berlin in the middle of the World War. In the absence of the regular trade union, and under conditions of martial law, the Revolutionaere Obleute, or Revolutionary Shop Stewards as they were called, planned and coordinated rank and file protests, slowdowns and strikes against their harsh working conditions and the rigors of the military regime. These were well-known, respected and trusted individuals who had long experience in trade union affairs. Their organization spread across Berlin heavy industry, and DMV locals throughout the Reich itself (Gluckstein 1985: 98-99; Von Oertzen 1963: 72). The most prominent among them was Richard Muller, a turner. In March 1916, despite the support of the majority, Muller had declined to challenge the conservative Adolph Cohen for the position of Berlin district leader in the metal workers union, probably because the assumption of such a high profile position would have almost certainly led to his arrest and the further involvement of the Obleute with the authorities (Gluckstein 1985: 99). Muller was described by a comrade as

> radical, efficient, possessing a healthy proletarian instinct. . . . with a diplomatic approach, he worked toward goals carefully and intelligently, removing all obstacles with tenacious energy. He was, within the DMV, a leader of the lathe operators, an advanced and extremely well organized group, and had acquired the complete trust of his workmates. (Schneider and Kuda 1969: 16)

Beginning with a core of some 50 to 80, the RO set about extending their organization by recruitment in different factories and other trades. Workers in the relatively new and unorganized industries, like chemicals, were often radicalized and more inclined to councils rather than trade unions, of which they had no experience. By the end of 1918, the Revolutionary Shop Stewards consisted of some several thousand. They constituted the hard core of the workers council movement (Gluckstein 1985: 98, 100; Brock 1978: 14; Arnold 1985: 70).

The first general strike in Berlin called by the Obleute was organized in defense of the Spartacist Karl Liebknecht, arrested at the anti-war rally in May 1916. On the occasion of his trial for treason the following month, some 55,000 workers from forty factories came out on strike for two days, chanting "Long Live Peace" and marching through the streets of Berlin in disciplined formations (Carsten 1982: 83). This was an an avowed political mass strike, remarkable in that it was able to be carried forward in an autocratic state under martial law. It also illustrates relative organizational strength within the German left at this period. While the Sparticist rally of political dissidents had attracted a few thousand, the Shop Stewards had turned out ten or fifteen times that number, occupied the streets, and had a major effect on war production for at least a few days. In Muller's view, "The first great mass strike won no apparent gains for the workers, but from a psychological point of view it did more than millions of leaflets and speeches" (Gluckstein 1985: 101).

Spontaneous, wildcat strikes became common through 1916 and 1917, despite the official characterization of them as criminal, treasonous activities. Throughout the war, Berlin managed to record the highest number of strikers of any industrial area in Germany (Ullrich 1987: 61-62; Gluckstein 1985: 92; Bock 1969: 82).

Following hard upon the severe "turnip winter," in March 1917 the authorities announced that the bread ration in Berlin would be cut by one quarter beginning April 15th, and that the extra food allotments given to those performing heavy labor would also be reduced. Leaflets quickly circulated throughout the factory districts demanding the end of the war and the overthrow of the Imperial government. Specific reference was made to the recent February Revolution in Russia that had toppled the Tsarist regime: "Our brothers, the Russian proletarians, four weeks ago were in the same boat. . . . (now) they have conquered freedoms of which the German worker does not dare to dream" (Carsten 1982: 124-125). To head off radical protest, Richard Muller was placed under military arrest. The DMV official Adolf Cohen immediately proposed the formation of special committees from the factories (hopefully under the control of the regular trade unions) to deal with the rationing problem (Carsten 1982: 125; Opel 1980: 59). But the union bureaucracy could not control events. Under pressure from the Revolutionary Obleute and responding to rank and file anger, the Berlin assembly of the DMV passed a resolution demanding increased rations, freedom for Muller and other political prisoners, a peace without annexations, and the lifting of the state of siege (Schneider and Kuda 1969: 18). On April 15th, delegates of the Berlin metal workers union voted to strike, joined by workplace committees and council delegates from other manufacturing plants the next day. Officials of the SPD and the Free Trade Unions briefly considered issuing an appeal against the strike, before deciding that such a move would constitute "political stupidity" (Carsten 1982: 125; Gluckstein 1985: 103).

The strike of April 16th brought out between 200,000 and 300,000 workers from hundreds of factories and workshops, with marches and demonstrations throughout the city and at workplaces. Trade union officials were shouted down or ignored. Besides increased supplies of food, the general demands now included peace, political and civil liberty and democratic electoral reform (Opel 1980: 59; Carsten 1982: 125-126). Most strikers returned to work two days later after promises of better distribution of rations, no loss of pay, and the eventual release of Richard Muller. In the wake of the strike, the military authorities took direct control of several armaments factories. Special military courts threatened fines and imprisonment for strikes and slowdowns. Yet working class discontent grew from week to week. (Carsten 1982: 126-129; Opel 1980: 60).

With the Imperial government now a virtual military dictatorship under the Generals Paul von Hindenburg and Erich Ludendorff, there was no intention of either reforming the government or initiating peace overtures. The authorities were confident that popular discontent could be controlled or suppressed, and that the war could still be successfully pursued to a German victory. The Russian Revolution in November 1917 and the subsequent Treaty of Brest-Litovsk with the Bolsheviks had the effect of encouraging both the conservative right and the socialist left— the former believing that reinforcements from the Russian front could tip the balance in the West, and the latter confident that peace and social revolution were now close at hand.

In December 1917 the military overseers were able to crush a strike at the Daimler works in Berlin. The metal workers threatened a general strike in the armaments industry in support of their comrades at Daimler, but in fact no action was taken (Carsten 1982: 129). But just a month later a massive walkout took place that far exceeded the previous mass actions of June 1916 and April 1917.

The immediate impetus for the Berlin strike of January 1918 was the outbreak of unrest in Austria. A cut in rations provoked a spontaneous general strike in Vienna which quickly spread to the other industrial areas of Austria and Hungary. Coincident wuth these events, a leaflet campaign had been carried on in Berlin calling on the workers to force the government to sue for peace. Sentiment grew in favor of a strike, and the Obleute, to cast a patina of legality over their activities, sought support from the Independent Socialist Reichstag delegation but most of the members were hesitant of provoking the Imperial authorities (Carsten 1982: 129-131; Opel 1980: 71). Nevertheless, on January 27th, Richard Muller and the Revolutionary Shop Stewards issued the call and brought out nearly 500,000 men and women. The following day, 414 delegates from the plants and workshops of the city convened at the Berlin trade union house. They elected 11 members of the Obleute to a strike committee, and formulated demands for the conclusion of peace with the active participation of the workers committee, abrogation of the Auxilliary Service Law and the state of siege, democratization of the state, amnesty for all political prisoners and an increase in the quantity and quality of food supplies (Carsten 1982: 132-133; Bailey 1980: 160). Friedrich Ebert, national secretary of the Majority SPD, attempted to attach himself to the strike committee with the intention, as he later admitted, of "bringing the strike to a speedy end to prevent damage to the country" (Gluckstein 1985: 106).

On the 29th, the strike committee sought a meeting with Imperial officials without success. The authorities regarded the delegates meeting at the trade union house to have been the constitution of a soviet "on the Russian pattern" (Carsten 1982: 133). With the police unable to control the streets, army troops were mobilized. On January 31st, the military command proclaimed a "severe state of siege" for Berlin and occupied seven major armaments plants. Any meetings of workers were banned, and strikers clashed with police and army units (Carsten 1982: 135; Bailey 1980: 163).

Now the government offered negotiation, but only if officials from the recognized trade unions were included. This the strike committee rejected and seeing no immediate alternative, voted to end the walkout on February 3rd, a week after it had begun (Carsten 1982: 135-136). Repression now began in full force. Some 50,000 strikers, mostly metal workers, were conscripted into the army, Richard Muller included. Many of them were sent to penal battalions (perhaps a major cause of the formation of soldiers and sailors councils some months later). Numbers of strikers were simply imprisoned (Bailey 1980: 163, 167). To all this the Social Democratic Party and the official trade unions made only formal protests (Bailey 1980: 163, 167, 169-170; Horn 1969: 55-58).

At this juncture the German left consisted of four major groupings. The Majority Socialists of the SPD and their allied Free Trade Unions had struck a partnership with the Imperial regime, and adhered to official policy, foreign and domestic. Within the ranks of the workers, they attempted to suppress any criticism of either themselves or the government, and preached patriotism and support for the war. The SPD split in 1916 with the expulsion of eighteen Reichstag deputies who rejected war credits, and this led to the formation of the Independent Socialist Party (Unabhaengige Sozialdemokratische Partei Deutschlands). The USPD was a diversified group held together by resistance to the war and Imperial plans of annexation, more a party of radical opposition than a revolutionary body. The Independent Socialists attracted between a quarter and a third of the regular SPD membership and was particularly strong in Berlin, where the Independents practically took over the local SPD organization (Morgan 1975: 67-70). There was a close connection between many of the USPD left and the Revolutionary Shop Stewards, with some overlapping membership (Morgan 1982: 308-309; Morgan 1975: 107, 122; Von Oertzen 1963: 71).

The Spartacist League led by Rosa Luxemburg and Karl Liebknecht, composed initially of the extreme left of the SPD, was theoretically and rhetorically at least the most radical of all. They constantly called for every strike and protest to be transformed into the social revolution. The Spartacists had few relatively few members in the factory ranks, being composed mainly of former SPD activists and intellectuals (Gluckstein 1985: 100-101). They drew the criticism of Richard Muller for their stridency and their "obsession with street action"; to "violently press the German working class for one action after another," he argued, "was damaging in itself and bad for the movement. The Spartakus League failed to recognize this fact" (Gluckstein 1985: 148, 101).

In Berlin and the other industrial cities, it was the Obleute, the Revolutionary Shop Stewards, who could claim to be the direct representatives of the working class. Delegates chosen from the same social stratum as those in whom name they spoke and acted, this group formed the core of the developing council movement. But with the overthrow of the autocratic regime, many workers and radicals would ignore the distinctions between these very different and opposing tendencies which had been formed under the pressure of wartime conditions. The new spirit of peace and unity that affected many leftists would help to revive the traditional Social Democratic Party and the Free Trade Unions, and enable them to contain and suppress the social revolution.

Chapter 8

Revolution

In September of 1918 the Allies penetrated the Hindenburg Line on the Western Front, and General Ludendorff advised the government to seek an armistice. The following month a constitutional monarchy was declared, and for the first time in German history, the Social Democrats were invited into the government. Cognizant of the political shift, and fearful of the popular mood, the German industrialists hastened to shore up their relations with the traditional labor organizations. Hans von Raumer of the Berlin electro-technical industry initiated talks between business leaders and the trade union hierarchy in the second week of October. As unrest increased, and it was feared that the unions might forfeit all influence and lose control of their members, the General Commission and management jointly agreed to procedures for the general demobilization and the provision of labor exchanges, the eight hour day, and the institution of industry-wide collective agreements. Coming when it did, this recognition by employers breathed life back into the traditional labor organizations (Moses 1982: 219-222).

At the beginning of November, revolutionary councils of sailors led mutinies in the Imperial fleet at the Kiel and Wilhelmshaven naval bases (Horn 1969: 220-266) Their example quickly spread and, against hardly any resistance, councils of workers and soldiers assumed power in one locality after the other across Germany. This was due perhaps less to the strength and coherence of the revolutionary movement than to the weakness of the old regime (Haffner 1986: 56-58; Kluge 1985: 59). Many such councils were actually composed of SPD and union functionaries with their own organizational agendas, skilled at the manipulation of public meetings. Usually only in the great cities and industrial areas like Berlin and Hamburg did the election of representative councils follow the pattern set by the mass strike committees of 1917 and 1918 (Muller 1971b: 57-78; Gluckstein 1985: 109-110; Comfort 1960: 41-46). Occupying the vacuum left by the disintegration of the Imperial order, it is not too much to claim that the councils at this point represented not merely workers and soldiers but also the mass of the war-weary German people.

The powers and functions of the councils varied from place to place, depending upon the composition of the membership, mode of selection and local circumstances. Of necessity, the councils immediately undertook to improvise a network of local and regional administration to deal with the vital problems of provisioning and demobilization. For these purposes alliances of convenience had to be made between the councils and local governmental administrations, political parties and unions. The general consciousness of mutual dependence of local groups one upon the other lessened political disagreements on all sides. In any case, most councils probably did not regard themselves as alternatives to a democratic, parliamentary system, but rather as auxiliaries to it (Kluge 1985: 59-60; Kolb 1962: 285-286).

The workers and soldiers councils of 1918 can be divided into two general groups, radical and democratic. The latter, usually with a high percentage of soldiers within their ranks, saw their organizations as temporary expedients that would function only until a constituent national assembly could be convened—an issue upon which the Social Democrats were most vocal. Those within the former type, mainly radicalized workers, advocated the augmentation and broadening of council power on a national basis. But the Leipzig council activist Kurt Geyer would later observe that "the possession of local power left the radical masses completely unable to see where the true distribution (of power) lay in the national structure" (Kolb 1962: 285, 292).

In "Red" Berlin, a general strike had been called for November 9th, to force the abdication of the Kaiser. The American spouse of a Prussian official noted the tumult in the streets in her diary:

> Across the compact masses of the moving crowd big military lorries urged their way, full to overflowing with soldiers and sailors, who waved red flags and uttered ferocious cries. They were evidently trying to excite the strikers to violence. These cars, crowded with young fellows in uniform or mufti, carrying loaded rifles or little red flags,

seemed to me characteristic. . . . About two hundred of these big lorries must have passed beneath our windows in two hours (Watt 1968: 197).

The plaza facing the Reich Chancellory, at the center of the city at the intersection of the Wilhelmstrasse and the Leipzigerstrasse, filled up with strikers and soldiers. Under popular pressure, and with reluctance, the Social Democratic ministers within proclaimed a republic. Friedrich Ebert now headed the state (Watt 1968: 193-197; Miller and Potthoff 1983: 65).

The Revolutionary Obleute had been planning for several weeks to launch a coup in Berlin on November 11th. Overtaken by events but determined to act, several hundred Shop Stewards, attracting followers from the streets, occupied the Reichstag on the evening of the 9th. In the main assembly chamber they issued a call to all factories and barracks to elect workers and soldiers delegates for a meeting the following afternoon at the Zirkus Busch. This meeting would elect a Council of People's Commissars, a provisional government, and there was to be no acknowledgement of the newly installed regime dominated by the SPD (Haffner 1986: 87-88). The liberal Count Harry Kessler visited the Reichstag that evening and recorded his impressions:

> In front of the main entrance, and in an arc of illumination provided by the headlights of several army vehicles, stood a crowd waiting for news. People pushed up the steps and through the the doors. Soldiers with slung rifles and red badges checked everyone's business. . . . The scene inside was animated, with a continual movement up and down the stairs of sailors, armed civilians, women and soldiers. The sailors looked healthy, fresh, neat and . . . very young; the soldiers old and war-worn, in faded uniforms and down-at-heels footwear, unshaven and unkempt, remnants of an army, a tragic picture of defeat. . . . Groups of soldiers and sailors stood and lay about on the enormous red carpet and among the pillars of the lobby.
>
> Rifles had been stacked. Here and there some individual was stretched full length and asleep on a bench. It was like a film of the Russian Revolution, a scene from the Tauride Palace in Kerensky's day. The door of the council chamber flew open. . . . A multitude swarmed among the seats, a sort of popular assembly, soldiers without badges, sailors with slung rifles, women, all of them with red arm-bands (Kessler 1971:7-8).

But the Majority Social Democrats moved very quickly to head off the radical coup. The next day, Ebert co-opted three USPD members into his cabinet, now renamed the Council of People's Representatives. One of the radicals, Emil Barth, was also a member of the Revolutionary Shop Stewards. And at the Zirkus Busch that afternoon, the Obleute could only muster about a quarter of the delegates. Calling for socialist unity and against fratricide, a large number of elected workers were SPD and official trade union supporters. Virtually all the military delegates, soldiers mostly from small towns and rural areas, backed the Majority Social Democrats. The twenty member Executive Council selected by a rough numerical parity, finally consisted of ten soldiers, five SPD members, and only five of the Shop Stewards nominees (Eyck 1967: 49; Muller 1971b: 53-54; Haffner 1986: 93-95, 96-100).

Finally, as if to seal the Social Democrat's success that day, Chancellor Ebert had a fateful telephone conversation that evening with the army chief General Wilhelm Groener. In what the general would later call a "pact" with the Chancellor, he offered military support for the new government in return for an active campaign and free hand against all forms of Bolshevism and the "councils nonsense." Ebert, quite relieved, was only too happy to agree (Haffner 1986: 100-101, 110-111; Carsten 1982: 227-228).

On November 11th the Armistice was signed, ending the war which a trade union official had claimed would solve the unemployment problem, and in which over 1,800,00 German soldiers were killed on the battlefield, and more than 4,200,000 wounded and maimed (Schneider and Kuda 1969: 16; Pelz 1987: 82-83).

On November 12th, Richard Muller wrote formally to Ebert on behalf of the newly elected Executive Council of the Berlin Arbeiter und Soldatenraete reiterating its right to "supervise" the work of his cabinet. Ebert did not bother to reply (Gluckstein 1985: 126). The relations between the Majority Social Democrats and the independent USPD members in Ebert's cabinet may be illustrated by the following exchange at the end of December. The radical People's Naval Division had clashed with government troops. A heated discussion followed among the "People's Representatives" over the responsibility for the order to attack the sailors:

Emil Barth (USPD and Obleute)—When I awoke on the 24th . . . my wife came in and told me, "They are firing artillery in Berlin." "Good grief no" I said, "surely it is the dustcarts being unloaded." At that moment my driver appeared.

Dr. Otto Landesburg (Majority Social Democrat)—So you have a chauffeur! I don't!

Barth—I have got to get right across Berlin every day . . .

Wilhelm Dittman (USPD)—Scheidemann (Majority Social Democrat) comes in by car every day from Steglitz too. I walk.

Landesburg—Well it looks like we are the only proletarians. (Taylor 1986: 12)

But if foundering politically, the November Revolution had only strengthened the council movement in the workplaces. A conservative newspaper complained that in the typical Berlin factory,

The workers arrive on time . . . read their newspapers and slowly begin work. This is interrupted by debates and meetings. The employers are as powerless as the managerial staff. All power is in the hands of the workers committees. On all questions ranging from the reconversion of the factory to peacetime production, the supply of labour, the employment of demobbed soldiers, the implementation of agreements, work methods, and sharing out of work, on all these the workers committees have the last word. (Gluckstein 1985: 134)

The militant Gustav Milkuschutz reported on the activities of his council in the Spandau munitions complex:

Our first measure was the takeover of the management of the factory. The directors appointed under the Imperial regime were dismissed. . . . The production of armaments was immediately halted. Conversion to the manufacture of railway equipment was started. . . . For the defense of the plant against reactionary forces we formed a workers guard of employees, stationed at key places in the factory and armed with machine guns. With the workers council controlling production we could always be sure that the factory will never again manufacture arms for a war of exploitation. The surest guarantee of this was the socialization of basic industry and the other great factories. (Institut fur Marxismus-Leninismus 1968:210-211)

An elected council of 11 manual and 8 white collar workers took over Spandau's management (Gluckstein 1985: 124). A worker from the Daimler plant reported to the council executive:

> We have abolished piecework. The workers now do all hiring and firing. Recently the Daimler company paid out 130,000 marks to shareholders. From now on we want these dividends for ourselves and measures such as the abolition of piecework will bring them in our direction. (Gluckstein 1985: 135)

Besides the spread of factory occupations, in many working class areas of Berlin the raete were taking over the functions of the municipal government. Despite the appointment of an Independent Socialist as city police chief, armed workers patrolled their own streets in Charlottenburg, Neukoln and other districts. The overthrow of the monarchy had brought no immediate or noticeable democratization to either the factory floor or the local community except what measures had been initiated by the workers themselves. The council movement now entered a more explicitly radical phase, with growing demand for the socialization of industry and council control (what Muller had called "supervision") over the functions of the state (Gluckstein 1985: 123-125; Watt 1968: 198; Arnold 1985: 58).

The worst fears of the SPD, not to mention the German industrialists, were being realized—"wilde Sozialismus," incipient Bolshevism. The official, now legally recognized, unions charged that the Arbeiterraete broke the unity of the working class. the councils included people who "know nothing at all about the nature of unions and socialism," and who couldn't be trusted with the fate of German workers. The general view in the Social Democratic Party and the union hierarchy was that the council movement was the product of unskilled, uneducated mass production workers with "primitive ideas" (Von Oertzen 1963: 268, 271).

German business leaders were anxious to come to terms quickly with the new socialist government and reinforce their agreement with the Free Trade Unions. It was vital to do so, as Jakob Reichert of the Association of German Iron and Steel Manufacturers made clear, in order to "save manufacturers from socialization and nationalization . . . and from approaching socialism." His opinion was shared by Adolph Cohen of the metal workers who reasoned that the unions "could not solve the economic problems on their own, without the entrepreneurs" (Schneider

1991: 132). Accordingly, on November 15th, the General Commission of the ADGB and the Central Association of the Employers of Germany together signed the Zentralarbeitsgemeinschaft (ZAG), an an extension of their earlier October agreement. The ZAG guaranteed labor the right of association, banned company unions, and established works committees in all enterprises of more than 50 employees. These committees were to be under the control of the trade unions (Schneider 1991: 132-133).

With the enthusiastic backing of the Ebert government, elections to the works committees were quickly arranged for November 23rd, with the participation of both blue and white collar employees voting for representation on equal terms. It was hoped that the inclusion of the white collar work force would have a conservative influence on the process. Although explicitly under the supervision of the official unions, in consultation and cooperation with management, many in the union hierarchy feared that even these bodies could somehow be "politicized" by radical elements (Schneider and Kuda 1969: 22-24). Regular union membership revived and soared by the end of 1918, with 2,800,000 nation-wide (Schneider 1991: 384).

Food supplies were running low in Berlin in the last month of 1918. The rate of infant death within a few days of birth was 30%. Unemployment was climbing as Berlin became a magnet for the jobless and displaced. Despite the efforts of the government to discourage migration, within a short time the city would house one quarter of all the nation's unemployed (Gluckstein 1985: 123; Franck 1920: 112-113).

As its revolutionary horizons were widening strategically, the Shop Stewards felt the need for more caution tactically. The "wild socialism" of factory occupations and workers militias could not have been more threatening to the employers and the government. Now the Berlin Council Executive and the Obleute acted as mediators in labor-management disputes. Richard Muller worked to forestall take-overs at several sites, advising the workforce to bide its time (Gluckstein 1985: 139-142). In the meantime Ebert warned the councils to stop the interventions and the "buffooneries" (Carsten 1972: 133).

The position of the workers councils in Berlin and the other large cities of Germany at this juncture was not comparable to that of the workers soviets in the Russian Revolution. In St. Petersburg and Moscow there had existed a situation of dual power—the only effective political actors being the soviets on the one hand, composed mostly of committed revolutionaries, and the relatively weak Provisional government on the other (Anweiler 1974: 138-141). Conditions in Germany were far more problematic. The Social Democratic government, ruling under the banner of "socialism," had at least the tacit support of the army, the industrialists, and most of the working class and the population at large. Not the least formidable was the huge governmental bureaucracy—national, provincial and local—which Ebert had left intact. At best conservative, and at worst deeply hostile to any manifestation of liberalism or socialism, this army of civil servants constituted a great counter-revolutionary reserve (Carsten 1972: 45).

On December 16th, the first German Congress of Workers and Soldiers Councils assembled in Berlin. On the streets outside, 250,000 demonstrated, demanding all power to the raete. If the Revolutionary Obleute still harbored any hopes for a program of radical action to be agreed upon by the national council movement, they were again disappointed. The majority of councils were committed only to the rather moderate reforms advocated by the Social Democratic Party. Of the 490 delegates—406 representing workers and 84 soldiers—298, a clear majority were followers of the SPD, and of this number 104 were fulltime party or trade union officials. The USPD had 101 seats, 51 delegates represented other groups, and only 49 identified themselves as members of arbeiterraete (Muller 1971b 203; Gluckstein 1985: 142). The most important question under discussion was whether to support the Ebert government's call for elections to a National Assembly. Representatives of the Shop Stewards like Ernst Daumig argued unsuccessfully that the two systems, parliamentary and councilist, could not co-exist, and that a social revolution could not be achieved within a bourgeois political structure. A halt to the progress of the revolution, of course, was what many delegates were consciously voting for. Elections for the National Assembly were approved and set for the middle of January, the question of socialization of industry and other matters to be considered by that body. The only radical proposal that was able to be accepted was a resolution for the complete overhaul of the army. Ignored by Ebert, it only had the effect of infuriating General Groener (Muller 1971b: 203-220; Haffner 1986: 113-15).

On Christmas Eve, fighting broke out at the Imperial stables occupied by the People's Naval Division and government troops. Although outnumbered and outgunned, the sailors were reinforced by armed civilians who exhorted the soldiers not to fire. The troops withdrew, much to the government's consternation (Watt 1968: 230-235; Haffner 1986: 116-125). "It cannot go on like this," Ebert is said to have kept repeating to his staff, "One simply cannot govern like this" (Haffner 1986: 125). In protest over the army's action, the Independent Socialists quit the government (Haffner 1986: 125). The question of who would govern could only be decided by force.

Despite what appeared to be a victory for the radicals, conservative forces were already on the move. Ebert appointed the right-wing Social Democrat Gustav Noske to the post of minister of defence, with the aim of suppressing the social revolution. "Someone must become the bloodhound," Noske remarked," I won't shirk the responsibility" (Watt 1968: 238-239). Since regular army troops had proven unreliable in being sent into action against workers or their former comrades, the Socialist government set about hiring volunteer private armies or Free Corp (Freikorp). These units were made up mostly of unemployed and rootless war veterans, usually of right-wing sympathies. One such unit, the Reichstag regiment, was recruited and paid by the SPD itself (Waite 1969: 14-16, 30-40; Regler 1959: 73). Hermann Goering would later characterize the Freikorp as "the first soldiers of the Third Reich" (Waite 1969: 264).

General Groener's plans for "restoring order" in Berlin had already been discussed with the government a few weeks before:

> It was a question of wrenching power from the workers and soldiers Councils in Berlin. . . . A day-to-day military plan had been elaborated. . . . the disarming of Berlin, clearing Berlin of Sparticists. . . . This plan had been formed throughout with Herr Ebert's knowledge and agreement. (Haffner 1986: 110-111)

Chapter 9

1919

The political tension in Berlin in January 1919 exploded in civil war. What was called "Spartacist Week" began on January 5th with the dismissal of the Independent Socialist, Emil Eichorn, from his post as chief of police. This may have been a calculated provocation (Frolich 1972: 285-287). The Obleute, the USPD and the Spartacists—now formally renamed as the Communist Party of Germany (KPD)—called a protest demonstration of several hundred thousand, many armed. With no particular plan the crowds moved on to occupy the offices of the SPD newspaper, other press buildings, and the railway stations.

Karl Liebknecht, over opposition from Rosa Luxemburg and other KPD colleagues, joined a Revolutionary Committee together with left-wing Independents and some elements of the Obleute. Although the Committee claimed to have "provisionally taken over the business of government," it made no attempt to seize state buildings. Its message to the workers and soldiers of Berlin was ambiguous, merely demanding the overthrow of the Ebert government (Haffner 1986: 129-132). A day or so later the Spartacists issued a manifesto calling for the installation of a council-republic (KPD 1971: 97-99). Muller, Daumig and other prominent Shop Stewards withdrew from the affair (Morgan 1975: 214). In the confused situation, more moderate USPD members offered to mediate between the insurgents and the government (Haffner 1986: 131-132, 134).

In the temporary power vacuum, the Berlin Council Executive found its voice:

> The workers council *will* use its revolutionary authority and no one will stand in its way. . . . In the large factories the workers council has

executive powers over production, wages and working conditions. . . . The workers council . . . will act as the management. It will supervise and intervene in all technical and financial matters [emphasis in original]. (Gluckstein 1985: 150)

But given the divisions among the Obleute, and the uncertainty displayed by the insurgents themselves, it is not suprising that the councils took on a defensive attitude throughout the rebellion. Franz Beiersdorf, an ex-sailor employed at the Siemens plant, described his workmates reaction to events:

> All comrades were of the opinion that emphasis must be put on the factory; each factory must be made a fortress in which collectivization could be carried through. It was suggested that I take charge of organizing military supplies to the factories so that when the time came . . . they could be defended. . . . I thought the slogan 'make every factory a fortress' was correct. . . . my colleagues wanted arms for they took the call for a National Assembly to be open treason to the achievements of the revolution. They demanded . . . 'All power to the workers and soldiers councils' until our major demand is won—collectivization of the big factories. (Gluckstein 1985: 150-151)

Mass assemblies rallied in factories and parks—40,000 from the AEG and Schwartzkopf complexes alone—to urge an end to the standoff and affirm the unity of all socialist parties. The People's Naval Division declared neutrality. The Communists officially withdrew from the Revolutionary Committee on January 10th, but it was too late to head off conflict (Morgan 1975: 216, 217; Haffner 1986: 137; Gluckstein 1985: 155). Dilatory tactics and indecision brought on disaster. On the morning of the 10th, Freikorp troops began to enter Berlin from the suburbs. They moved immediately on the two insurgent strongpoints, the Belle-Allianz-Platz, housing the capital's leading newspapers, including the SPD's *Vorwaerts*, and the Spandau factory district. Forces were probably equally matched in numbers, with less than 10,000 on each side, but the Freikorp outgunned the defenders, being equipped with heavy machine guns, flame throwers, trench mortars and artillery. By January 11th, Berlin had been pacified, some rebel prisoners summarily shot on the spot. Sixty machine guns were deployed at the Spandau munitions plant and the workers literally driven back to work at gunpoint (Waite 1969: 60-62; Gluckstein 1985: 154-155). On January 15th, the fugitive

Spartacists Karl Liebknecht and Rosa Luxemburg were arrested, beaten and shot by Freikorp troopers (Frolich 1972: 299-300).

In the National Assembly elections held on January 19th, and boycotted by the KPD, the Majority Social Democrats won 165 seats, making them the largest party with nearly 38% of the total, while the USPD mustered only 22, about 7%. Parties of the center and right polled a majority between them. The Assembly selected Friedrich Ebert to be President of the Republic (Watt 1968: 275-278; Miller and Potthoff 1983: 71).

But the imposition of order on Berlin and the return to politics as usual did nothing to end hardship and privation in the city. A German-American visitor in early 1919 could not help setting down his impressions:

> That Berlin was hungry was all too evident. . . . Most of Germany was hungry, but Berlin was so in a superlative degree. . . . Loose-fitting clothing, thin, sallow faces, prominent cheekbones, were the rule among Berliners. . . . There was a suggestion of the famine victims of India in many German faces, particularly among the poor . . . in factory districts. (Franck 1920: 113, 137, 138, 139)

The last months of 1918 and the early weeks of January 1919 had seen the high tide of political power for the workers council organizations of Berlin. They would never again regain such direct influence over government policy. But the events of Spartacist Week and the National Assembly electoral campaign had done essentially nothing to uproot the councils from their grassroots bases in the workplaces and industrial plants. Organized face to face on the factory floor, the raete had originated and had flourished under repressive conditions.

Following the debacle of the Revolutionary Committee, relations with the other radical groups became further strained. The KPD called a strike on January 20th to protest the murders of Luxemburg and Liebknecht, and in some cases sent armed supporters into factories to force the workers out. it was the kind of tactic that the exasperated Richard Muller called "revoutionary gymnastics" (Kolb 1962: 293; Muller 1971a: 21-24). Within the USPD, charges were made that the Obleute were attempting to supercede the revolutionary party by fostering belief in a pure council system (Von Oertzen 1963: 79). Indeed, this was now true.

In the wake of the revolutionary defeats of the previous weeks, the Shop Stewards and council militants retreated back into their workplaces.

The recent events prompted a revival of radical thought and debate in the circles of the extreme left. There was a return to the economic concerns that had been pushed into the background in the heat of the revolutionary moment (Von Oertzen 1963: 79-80).

Despite the suppression of their organizations and their press at the outbreak of the war, the anarcho-syndicalists of Berlin had managed to maintain communication between themselves and their comrades throughout the Reich, clandestine activity in which the Berlin construction worker Fritz Kater was prominent. These elements naturally gravitated toward the Arbeiterraete. And the traditional syndicalist conception of the revolutionary union as the basic unit of workers power and autonomy began to give way to the new ideas of the council movement and factory-based organization (Bock 1969: 83, 85-87; Souchy 1976; Von Oertzen 1963: 97).

By February of 1919, councilist pamphlets and periodicals made their appearance, the weekly *Die Arbeiter-Rat* (The Workers Council) and others. Within their pages the internal discussion proceeded, as the council movement became more conscious of itself as a new and distinct kind of socialist movement with its own ideology and program, even as an alternate system of governance apart from traditional state and party structures (Von Oertzen 1963: 70, 79; Morgan 1982: 315). The leading councilist theorectician was the journalist Ernst Daumig, a former non-commissioned officer in both the French Foreign Legion and the German army, who had been an editor of the Social Democratic *Vorwaerts* and a lecturer in the party's worker education program. Of those prominent in the raete movement, he was one of the few intellectuals to have the acceptance and trust of the Revolutionary Obleute (Morgan 1982: 304-306; Schneider and Kuda 1969: 21).

The great upheavals shaking the postwar world, Daumig believed, offered the opportunity to reconstruct a new and just society upon the ruins of the old. In this new order, merely formal, parliamentary democracy had no place. It simply perpetuated the traditional social relations of exploitation and domination of one class by another under a different facade. The question was not how to fit the workers councils into the framework of bourgeois democracy in some sort of subordinate position to capital. The real question was the choice between sham liberal democracy or direct, popular democracy through the workers councils (Morgan 1982: 310-311; Daumig 1969: 94; Daumig 1971: 82-83). Only the council system made it possible to place all social, economic and political questions under the direct control of the rank and file. For this it required the full participation of all workers, whether they toiled by hand or by brain. It was necessary therefore to awaken them from the old habits of thought and behavior, to shake off the weight of the past; as Daumig insisted,

> The German proletariat has neither a revolutionary tradition nor revolutionary temperament because the German proletariat is infected right into its class-conscious ranks with the spirit of subjection in which rhe German people have been raised for generations. (Morgan 1982: 313)

These inclinations were reinforced by the Social Democracy under whose tutelage,

> The organized masses (were) drilled on party discipline, punctual payment of dues . . . the organization itself a rigid, bureaucratically elaborated structure. . . . The (trade union) leaders almost exclusively dominated by the reformist outlook . . . without in any way threatening the private profit economy of capitalism. (Morgan 1982: 313)

The workers councils were not the result of a preconceived ideology or a party program but rather were structures born of necessity within a context of war and revolution. Such workers organizations had made their appearance during the Paris Commune, and the first and second Russian Revolutions. The German councils were of a similar character. Councilism was "practical socialism," not necessarily a fixed and eternal system but a social organism capable of developing and adapting itself as conditions might demand. The functioning of the arbeiterraete was synonymous with the conscious and active participation of the proletariat at large, exercising direct control at their workplaces over their elected council representatives. Finally, the councils could not be the preserve of a single party or group, but had to embrace the entire working class (Daumig 1969: 65-70).

March of 1919 saw more bloody "revolutionary gymnastics." Once again the Spartacists called for a general strike, this time urging the workers to remain inside their factories and to avoid street fighting. When Noske's Free Corps returned to Berlin, they were resisted by the remnants of the People's Naval Division whom the Spartacists now refused to support. Nevertheless, in the confusion Spartacist supporters defended the police headquarters before retreating into the proletarian neighborhoods of east Berlin. To the usual array of superior firepower the government forces now added aerial bombardment. Noske decreed death for anyone bearing arms against the government, an order to which the Freikorps gave quite liberal interpretation. Some 1200 to 1500 Berliners were kiled, including 300 unarmed sailors of the Naval Division (Waite 1969: 69-77; Haffner 1986: 161-162).

The Majority Socialist *Vorwaerts* editorialized that it was only natural that the Volunteers (Free Corps) should fulfill their duty with "resolute firmness" (Waite 1969: 77). Indeed, throughout 1919 the Freikorps displayed such "firmness" in the suppression of workers and soldiers councils and leftist outbreaks throughout the Reich, in Bremen, Munich and elsewhere (Waite 1969: 66-68, 79-93; Carsten 1972: 153-155, 161-164).

In April of 1919, the second and last national congress of workers and soldiers councils met in Berlin. Again, the Social Democrats had a majority of the delegates. The Independent Socialists and councilists denounced the Ebert-Noske use of the Frei Korps at the same time that the SPD called for socialist unity, i.e. support for that very policy. But the popular consensus among the working class for socialization of industry and the wide influence of the factory councils could not be ignored by the Social Democrats. Ebert's Minister for Economic Affairs, Rudolf Wissell, had to explain that large-scale socialization of German industry was impossible because of the nation's economic plight (Carsten 1972: 140-141). Observing the proceedings, Count Kessler noted the following impressions in his diary:

> Germany's deplorable situation, he (Wissell) protested, renders far-reaching socialization impossible. As I see it, socialization either increases production, in which case this is the time to implement it, or diminishes it (as Wissell clearly assumes) and should therefore never be undertaken. The objection can be raised that Germany is not economically ruined, but that the workers, as a result of the war, do not want to work any longer. But why should they work less in socialized enterprise than they do now? This seems to me an extremely weak line of defense, especially coming from a Social Democrat. (Kessler 1971: 94)

A large minority of delegates supported Daumig's proposal for a "pure" council system to replace capitalism and the traditional state (Arnold 1985: 58).

Two months later the first postwar congress of the Free Trade Unions convened at Nuremburg. The General Commission was anxious to align itself in a national partnership with the employers and the government, while at the same time diluting the power of the workers councils and bringing them under the control of the traditional trade unions. Carl Legien asserted that the workers were "disappointed" with the councils, and their only effect was to "hinder the work of the trade unions and the community of workers." For these purposes the creation of works councils with limited but recognized workplace functions was advocated. These would operate as extensions of the unions and would not have as their aim the control of industry or political power (Schneider 1991: 135; Opel 1980: 82-83).

Richard Muller, representing the Berlin metal workers, rejected the Commission's proposal. Instead he outlined his plan for a council system organized along federal lines. The coexistence of a vital council system with a bourgeois parliament could not long continue and would be a source of "continuous turmoil." The future of the German working class, he argued, depended upon all political and economic power devolving upon the councils. A Social Democrat countered that any sort of socialization would be impossible in a Germany surrounded by hostile capitalist nations. The General Commission's proposal was accepted over Muller's by a vote of 407-192 (Schneider 1991: 135; Moses 1982: 283-287; Opel 1980: 83).

If the basic hard core of council strength in the industrial complexes of Berlin and elsewhere in Germany were able to endure if not conquer, they found themselves in increasing competition for the allegiance of their working class constituency. Trade union membership soared in the early months of 1919 as demobilized soldiers and previously unorganized employees flocked to join trade unions. Membership by year's end stood at over 7,300,000 compared to some 1,500,000 in 1914 (Schneider 1991: 151-153, 384). this was attributed to the legal recognition, and even tacit encouragement, of the established trade unions on the part of government and management, and to the rising expectations of many working people following the end of the war and the overthrow of the monarchy.

The inability of the "pure" council movement to dominate the workers councils movement at large, much less the trade union organizations, was due to the great attachment, active or passive, that many workers felt towards the regular Social Democracy and its allied trade unions. Far from constituting an ideologically homogenous mass, it appears that most workers were either indifferent or confused by the various sectarian divisions within the German Left. Even many of those who participated in the workplace councils—at least outside of Berlin—were members or adherents of the SPD, and did not regard the councils as alternates to the party or the Free Trade Unions, but rather as subordinate to them. They expected that those established and now legally recognized institutions would carry out and implement the necessary political and economic reforms. In addition, some militants were lost to the Spartacists, for whom the councils were merely organs of class struggle—preferably armed—which would help their party to seize state power (Souchy 1976).

Nevertheless the councilists continued to flex their muscles. At the Social Democratic Party conference at Weimar in June, Hugo Sinzheimer lectured his party comrades on the basic impetus behind the councils:

> It would be false to suppose that the movement is some sort of premediated strategy, or imitation of the Russian example, In reality the council movement has domestic . . . sources . . . the masses felt that despite the political revolution their daily lives had not changed. The old social apparatus remained in place. To this disappointment was added the expectations aroused by the revolution. . . . The people wanted to create a new life for themselves to control their own destiny and not be exploited for someone else's purposes . . . that is the basis of the council movement among them. (Schneider and Kuda 1969: 34)

In July at the Siemens complex, the workers council demanded that the facility be shut down to allow the employees to attend an anti-capitalist demonstration. The management fired 42 shop stewards outright, and 30,000 workers struck for five days until they were reinstated. With new council elections in the Berlin factories slated for mid-August, Ebert and Noske decided to take action. The office of the Berlin executive council was closed by troops and further workplace elections forbidden (Opel 1980: 93; Morgan 1975: 269).

On August 11th the Weimar constitution was adopted by the National Assembly. Under the pressure of popular support for socialization of industry, and the continuing activities of the arbeiterraete, the constitution contained specific references to works councils. Article 165 provided for the creation of works councils in factories, open to all, whether union members or not (Moses 1982: 302; Umbreit 1978: 178). A "spirit of concurrence" with the employer was to be fostered, and the Article further declared that,

> the worker has an immediate interest in his workplace and the public good; in participation in the process of production. No longer is the worker merely confined to regular tasks and work practices, but will be able to view the workings of the economy as a whole. The worker will now use his expertise and experience in his participation in productive development. The combination of efforts inspires the whole labor force. (Umbreit 1978: 178)

The works councils were to take on an active role in the advancement of production, but employee participation should not infringe upon managerial direction of the workplace (Umbreit 1978: 179). Thus as the trade union leadership had hoped, the trend begun with the Auxiliary Service Law during the war had continued, and the trade unions were now legally integrated into German society after decades of outlaw status.

The works committees were legally empowered to negotiate with management over wages and conditions of labor. They were designed to be allied and subordinate to the established unions. While welcomed by the latter, there was however fear that radical elements would be able to infiltrate the new organizations. And soon enough this began to occur, as some works councils attempted to assert control of enterprise management (Moses 1982: 309-310, 312-314, 319). In Berlin, councilists went further and formed an Independent Works Council bureau to which 26,000 works councils affiliated. Militance was encouraged and the wildcat strike advanced as a tactic. A meeting of German employers in the capital condemned the new laws as "dangerous to production, order and efficiency in the workplace." In September metal workers struck at Siemens and Borsig over wage rates. The strike was immediately suppressed by troops with some street fighting. The metal workers union, the DMV, protested that the strikes were not political, but "purely economic disputes' that did not require government intervention. (Moses 1982: 314-315; Opel 1980: 94-95). Berlin's "wild socialism" had yet to be tamed.

By the summer of 1919, the councilists had begun to recognize the trade unions as the great barrier to radical organization in the workplace. They correspondingly shifted all their efforts from the political to the economic sphere, the classic practice of anarcho-syndicalism. The council advocates considered that the further development of a conscious mass revolutionary movement would depend upon education and concentration upon the struggles of everyday work life, just as the councils themselves had their origins in the privations of the working class during the World War. But at that time the unions had essentially abandoned the workers to the discipline and direction of the state authorities, leaving the field to the Revolutionary Shop Stewards. Now the unions were back, with considerable resources and the support of the national government, if not the employers (Arnold 1985: 95-96; Opel 1980: 92).

The Independent Socialist and councilist caucuses within the major unions were still sizeable. And the opposition won its greatest victory in this period at the metal workers national conference in October, when radicals were elected to the union executive. Richard Muller was installed as editor of the *Metall-Arbeiter-Zeitung* (Metal Workers News) (Morgan 1975: 271-272). "We want," he wrote,

> First of all to set up the economic mechanism of the council system, the political mechanism will follow, if the first has been established. The political aspect of the system is as important as the economic, but it will not be possible to do both at the same time. (Opel 1980: 84)

But it soon became increasingly difficult for councilists to function within the trade union environment. Robert Dissman, newly elected chairman of the metal workers, was a prominent member of the USPD and had been an advocate of the arbeiterraete. But in office he soon found himself inadvertently calling for the extension of the powers of the works councils, a development that strengthened the position of the traditional trade unions in the workplace. "Pure" councilism had become difficult to sustain in practice.

Dissatisfied with the results of a wage arbitration, the Berlin metal workers threatened industry-wide walkouts in early November. Sentiment for a general strike in support of the DMV began to grow, and was advocated by the Greater Berlin executive of the arbeiterraete, the USPD and the Communists. Gustav Noske warned on November 7th that agitation for a general strike was "an immediate danger to public safety and order," a remark obvious in its implications. Under conflicting pressures the General Commission split 66 to 66 over support for a general strike, with the result that no action was taken. The original arbitration award was upheld, a victory for the employers. Richard Muller only lasted six months as editor of the DMV newsletter (Moses 1982: 315; Morgan 1975: 272; Opel 1980: 96).

Chapter 10

1920

Through the end of 1919 and the beginning of the new year the National Assembly debated the Ebert government's Factory Council Law. In an effort to minimize radical influences on the works councils and to placate employers, this measure aimed at modifying Article 165 of the Constitution and curtailing and specifiying the powers of the works committees. White and blue collar employees would now be organizationally separate, elections would be held at regular intervals rather than at the workers' will, the works councils and committees would not be allowed to federate either industrially or regionally. Further, the bill declared all other such organizations, such as the arbeiterraete, illegal. Only a restricted works council would have legal recognition. (Morgan 1975: 311-312).

While industrial unrest spread across Germany, the central office of the Berlin workers councils, along with the USPD and the Communists, called for a mass protest demonstration against the Council Law in front of the Reichstag on January 13th. As the large crowd moved toward the entrances to the building at the end of the rally, the police opened fire and shot down 42 demonstrators, wounding 105 more. Berlin was again placed under a state of siege (a condition which had prevailed most of the time since the November Revolution). Noske began a systematic repression against the oppositionist Left, while the new Factory Council legisiation passed into law (Morgan 1975: 314-315, 319).

Meanwhile, right-wing elements were plotting the overthrow of the republic, incensed by the constant armed outbreaks, strikes and leftist agitation, and by the acquiescence of the Ebert and his cabinet (the "November criminals") to the hated Versailles Treaty. In March the East Prussian official Wolfgang Kapp led a coup d'etat attempt in the capital, with the support of several Freikorp units and military officers. The regular national army, the Reichwehr, declined to intervene against the rebels and the government fled. Immediately, the call for a general strike went out from the SPD and the Free Trade Unions, and all of the radical groups (except, initially, the Communists). The strike was joined by the liberal and Catholic trade unions, and support for the general strike even reached into the ranks of the higher civil service—nominally a conservative constituency. All services and commerce, public and private, ceased throughout Berlin, including electrical utilities and newspaper publishing. Within a few days, Kapp and his clique withdrew, but not before several hundred Berliners had been shot by Freikorp troopers, further inflaming the hatred of workers for the military (Eyck 1967: 148-152; Kessler 1971: 121).

There had been two general strike committees in Berlin during the Kapp putsch attempt, one formed by the Social Democrats and the ADGB, and the other composed of the USPD and the representatives of the arbeiterraete. With the renewed wave of popular feeling against the government and the military, Berlin radicals attempted to prolong the general strike to force the installation of at least a more authentically leftist government. Some in the SPD also saw an opportunity. Carl Legien demanded that the unions be granted "decisive influence . . . on the reconstruction of the government of the Reich and the states and the development of new legislation in economics and social policy." Specifically Legien asked for the purge of the "political and economic administration of all reactionary elements," the dissolution of the Free Corps and the socialization of power production (Miller and Potthoff 1983: 89-90; Morgan 1975: 327). He approached the USPD with proposals for a common front, but these efforts were frustrated by the right wing of the SPD and the left wing of the Independents (Morgan 1975: 327-331). Even with these developments, and miners in revolt in the Ruhr, the general strike could not be sustained, as the central office of the Berlin councils acknowledged at the beginning of April (Morgan 1975: 331-337; Waite 1969: 172-182). An Independent Socialist noted that "however much the movement progressed intellectually, in the greater part of Germany the proletariat still lacked the energy to elect independent factory councils extralegally against (the will of) the employer" (Morgan 1975: 319). The government of Ebert remained in power.

Richard Muller, Ernst Daumig and other council militants now took the lead in attempting to revive the weakening council movement by opening the Munz Street Center in Berlin as a kind of clearinghouse of information, education and propaganda for the arbeiterraete. The Center declared that its most important task was,

> To unite all the strength of the working people in one fighting organization and to decide upon the necessary economic and political actions to take . . . (to) preserve the direction of the economic struggle from control by the inept union leadership. (Brigl-Mathis 1978: 27-28)

It would be, however, the councils last effort at survival. Through the summer of 1920 the struggle between raete and the unions for control of the legally instituted works councils system intensified. Writing in *Der Arbeiterrat*, Daumig insisted that,

> The factory councils (must) take from the law everything that can be taken from it, and that, supported and driven on by the working masses behind them, they (must) prepare the way for socialism in the production process, without regard for the limiting clauses (of the law). (Morgan 1975: 346)

The close relationship that had always existed between the left wing of the USPD and the councilists now became a disadvantage in the competition with the trade unions. Many workers, radical or not, were hostile to any aspect of interference by political parties in union affairs (Morgan 1975: 347). On their part, trade union officials considered control of the works committees to be a "question of life and death." They were adamant that "in order to put the activity of the factory councils at the service of the community . . . the factory councils are to be built into the overall organization of the trade unions" (Morgan 1975: 346). By autumn the trade union leadership felt confident enough to call for a conference of the legal works councils. On October 20th, some three-quarters of the works committee delegates opted for control of their organizations by the trade unions (Morgan 1975: 346; Brigl-Mathis 1978: 30). The following month, the Berlin regional trade union commission, under heavy pressure from the national leadership, voted 93—30 to break off all relations with the workers councils and their Munz Street Center (Brigl-Mathis 1978: 39).

Thereafter, at the first conference of the works councils of the metal workers union, the general secretary Robert Dissmann, a long time advocate of the arbeiterraete, declared that "Developments have forced us to acknowledge the fact that the autonomous council organizations have almost completely disappeared" (Brigl-Mathis 1978: 40).

Chapter 11

Council Communism

If traditional German culture was to a great extent authoritarian, the revolution and civil strife of these years had radicalized hundreds of thousands of workers, and contributed to the rise of an antiauthoritarian movement on the Left. As the factory arbeiterraete found their viability ebbing away under the pressures of trade union competition, government repression, employer hostility and legal restriction, new, formal organizations of anarcho-syndicalists and councilists were constituted. Although divided along sectarian lines, they shared a common radical program—antiauthoritarian, antiparlimentary and antimilitarist, with the emphasis upon direct action on the shop floor (Morgan 1975: 346-347; Bock 1990: 63-64). These groups inherited the activists and ideologues of the prewar syndicalist movement, the union localists, factions of the left wing of the Social Democracy and many of the original Obleute and councilists. The "Raeteideen" persisted in these mass movements (Souchy 1976).

The Free Labor union of Germany (Freie Arbeiter-Union Deutschland—FAUD) was founded in December 1919 in Berlin out of the remnants of the old Free Association of German Trade Unions (FVdG), newly radicalized elements, and anarcho-syndicalists like Rudolf Rocker and Augustin Souchy recently returned from exile. Although consciously syndicalist and regarding itself as a revolutionary union similar to the American IWW, the FAUD embraced the idea of workers councils (Souchy 1976; Rocker 1985: 17), Headquartered in Berlin, the FAUD was particularly strong among the miners of the Ruhr. There arose considerable friction between these two centers. The Berlin office was charged with bureaucraticism, and the organization finally split along regional lines (Bock 1969: 167-187; Freie Arbeiter Union 1986: 13). Through 1921 the union maintained a membership of over 100,000 (Freie Arbeiter Union 1986: 9-10; Gerhard 1972: 51). For the next several years at least, the FAUD was able to compete rather successfully in the elections for works councils. it also addressed itself to cultural issues and published no less than 71 periodicals of various types on a national and regional level (Bock 1990: 74-75).

The beginning of 1920 saw the formation of the General Workers Union of Germany (Allgemeine Arbeiter Union Deutschlands—AAUD) in which former members of the left wing of the KPD played a large role. It appears that the remaining hard core activists of the council movement were attracted to the AAUD, with some also in contact with the FAUD. It was about this time that. the term "council communism" came into parlance, possibly in part so that Marxists could distinguish themselves from traditional anarcho-syndicalists. The AAUD completely boycotted traditional trade unionism and the legal works committees. By the end of 1920, it claimed a membership of 300,000, some 30,000 of which in Greater Berlin. Soon enough, about a third of the membership left in a dispute over "pure" councilism and politics and formed the United AAUD (AAUD—Einheitsorganisation) (Meijer 1972: 6-7; Shipway 1987: 108; Bock 1990: 195). The AAUD defined its basic goal as "factory organization, class organization, leading to council organization" (Arnold 1985: 162).

The third major group of the German antiparliamentary Left was the Communist Workers Party of Germany (Kommunistischen Arbeiter-Partei Deutschlands—KAPD), founded by dissidents from the Bolshevised Communist Party in Berlin in April of 1920 (Bock 1969: 225-229). Claiming an orthodox Marxist pedigree, the KAPD condemned the "counterrevolutionary institutions" of parliament, trade unions and legalized works councils (Reichenbach 1994: 137-138). Calling itself the "determined vanguard of the proletariat," the organization declared that,

> The KAPD is not a party in the traditional sense. It is no leadership party. Its main work will be helping the German proletariat to its utmost on its way to liberation from every leadership. Liberation from treacherous, counterrevolutionary leadership—politics is the most effective method for the unification of the proletariat in the spirit of council thought. (Roy 1970: 18b)

The close relations between the KAPD and AAUD had provoked the split in the latter organization (Riesel 1981: 278). The Communist Workers Party attracted nearly 40,000 adherents, and at that time, with some 12,000 members, was stronger in the Berlin area than the KPD itself (Meijer 1972: 10-11; Roy 1970: 18; Bock 1969: 239).

Despite its declarations, there was some ambiguity within the KAPD as to the exact function of the party in the struggle for workers councils. Was it to take a leading role? Opinions were mixed (Riesel 1981: 277-278; Mattick 1978: 106-107). Expressing perhaps a traditional Social Democratic current in the party, Hermann Gorter asserted that,

> Most proletarians are ignoramuses. They have little notion of economics or politics. . . . By reason of their position in society they cannot get to know all this. This is why they can never act at the right moment. . . . They repeatedly make mistakes. (Meijer1972: 12)

On this point at least, Gorter's views were quite consistent with Lenin and the Russian Bolsheviks, who maintained that "there could not be socialist consciousness among the workers. This consciousness could only be brought to them from without. . . . the working class, exclusively by its own effort, is able to develop only trade union consciousness" (Lenin 1972: 16-17; Souchy 1992: 30-31; Brendel 1973).

Conversely however, the KAPD activist Otto Ruehle asserted that,

> The concept of a party with a revolutionary character in the proletarian sense is nonsense. . . . The councils system is the organization of the proletariat corresponding to the nature of class struggle. . . . If Marx said that the working class could not simply take over the government machine of the capitalist state, but must find its own form for carrying out its revolutionary task, this problem is solved in the councils organization. (Ruehle 1974: 26, 52)

With the independent KAPD a serious rival to the Moscow-controlled German Communist Party, Lenin himself set out to chastise the Marxist dissidents. His well-known polemic *Left-Wing Communism: An Infantile Disorder* (1969) was written specifically with the KAPD in mind as he castigated the "pseudo-revolutionaries" of the extreme left, exalted the discipline of the Bolshevik "vanguard" and argued for radical participation in parliament and the trade unions. In his reply, Hermann Gorter lectured the Bolshevik leader on the differences between the industrialized West and Tsarist Russia, and asserted that the trade unions had to be "destroyed and replaced by industrial associations based on factory and workshop organizations. . . . The workers need weapons for the revolution in Western Europe. The only weapons are the factory organizations" (Gorter 1967: 234).

The so-called March Action of the German Communist Party in 1921 was reminiscent of the earlier "revolutionary gymnastics" of the Spartacists in Berlin which had so frustrated and baffled the Obleute. As a KPD member would later describe it, "the party went into battle without concerning itself over who would follow it" (Morgan 1975: 398). The call of the KPD for an armed revolution was a confused affair, generally restricted to central Germany—where the anarcho-syndicalist Max Hoelz and a workers militia successfully battled government troops for a few weeks (Gruber 1967: 315). In Berlin the armed elements of the KAPD participated in the uprising and did most of the street fighting (Roy 1970: 23). KPD headquarters in the capital supplied no clear orders, and In some areas the Communists attempted to force apathetic workers to leave their factories (Gruber 1967: 315; Roy 1970: 23). The Communist attempt to achieve a revolutionary breakthrough by sheer force of will was a disaster. The repression that followed fell not only upon the KPD but on the entire German Left (Roy 1970: 23; Gruber 1967: 315; Arnold 1985: 182).

Not only the radicals were frustrated. The labor-management cooperation touted by the SPD and the Free Trade Unions began to brake down under growing employer intransigence. Wage and hour negotiation generally brought no tangible results. Strikes were being lost at an increasing rate. Membership plummeted and the unions lost 4 million members by the mid-twenties (Schoenhoven 1987: 124-125; Schneider 1991: 385). Apathy and resignation among workers followed the bloody repressions of the revolutionary years. Human endurance had its limits (Souchy 1976).

With revolutionary prospects dimmed, and the rank and file factory organizations unable to function as viable means of struggle and representation, numbers of council activists shrank, while the KPD, heavily subsidized by Moscow and relying on the prestige of the Russian Revolution, became the third largest party in Germany by the early 1930s—exceeded only by the Social Democrats and the growing National Socialist movement. The council communists and anarcho-syndicalists were eventually reduced to several thousand (Bock 1990: 70; Meijer 1972:

14; Reichenbach 1994: 142). Their activities became mainly restricted to propaganda and discussion, although the militants of the FAUD remained active in the works councils (Mattick 1978: 107-108; Bock 1990: 74). In writing of the AAUD, Anton Pannekoek noted that,

> The AAUD, like the KAPD, is essentially an organization whose immediate goal is the revolution. In other times, in a period of decline of the revolution, one could not have thought of founding such an organization. But it has survived the revolutionary years; the workers who founded it before and fought under its flag do not want to let themselves lose the experience of these struggles and conserve it like a cutting from a plant for the developments to come. (Meijer 1972: 15)

Chapter 12

Conclusion

The appearance of the movement of workers councils in Berlin was the direct result of the hardship and deprivations of life and the exploitation of labor suffered by industrial workers under a dictatorial regime in wartime conditions. After decades of radical propaganda, these workers were abandoned by the socialist party and the trade unions, long the traditional organizations of the German proletariat, and were thrown back upon their own resources. Acting from the immediacy of their own experience, and the practical necessity of defending their living standards and working conditions, the workers of Berlin were able to create rank and file councils and assemblies in their factories and workshops based upon direct democracy and elemental solidarity. In their workplaces and neighborhoods they attempted, so far as they could, to implement those principles of democracy and equality that Social Democratic politicians and union officials had told them would only be possible in the socialist utopia of the indefinite future. For many, the workers councils became a viable alternative to the capitalist economic system and the established political order, the cells of a future self-managed society.

The existence of the autonomous councils provides a living contradiction to the Leninist dogma that revolutionary consciousness can only be brought to working people from outside their class, i.e. by middle class intellectuals. as the revolutionary veteran and council theorist Paul Mattick has observed:

> The German working class was a highly socialistically educated working class, quite able to conceive of a social revolution for the overthrow of capitalism. Moreover, it was not 'revolutionary conscious-

ness' that the middle class intellectuals had carried into the working class, but only their own reformism and opportunism. . . . Marxist revisionism did not originate in the working class, but in its leadership, for which trade unionism and parliamentarism were the sufficient means for a progressive social development. (1978: 278)

Indeed the councils found themselves caught on the one hand between the conservative reformism of the Majority Social Democrats, who did not hesitate to employ force to suppress "wild socialism," and the sporadic and ill-conceived uprisings of the Spartacists and Communists on the other.

In those years of social upheaval and economic crisis, the Berlin arbeiterraete were part of a widespread and unprecedented councilist movement that swept across Germany, and from one end of Europe to the other, Tsarist Russia to rural Ireland. But the workers councils of Berlin proved to be the most highly developed, the most conscious of purpose, perhaps the most durable and memorable of all.

The experience of the Berlin working class can be seen in the context of such social phenomena throughout the twentieth century. Revolutionary councils and committees of rank and file workers have appeared as mass movements in the factories of St. Petersburg and Moscow in 1905 and 1917, during the Spanish Revolution in the mid-1930s, in Budapest in 1956, in the May Days of '68 in France, in Chile, Portugal and Tehran in the following decade, and most recently in the Polish Solidarity union of the 1980s. Apparently endemic to industrial society, they are, as Staughton Lynd has noted, "the horizontal, decentralized organizational forms based on solidarity, which . . . explode from within the working class in moments of crisis" (1997: 231).

Appendix A

Chronology

1890
- Repeal of the Anti-Socialist Law

1891
- Social Democratic Party officially adopts a Marxist program at the Erfurt Congress
- Founding of the DMV, the metal workers union

1897
- Localists and anarcho-syndicalists form Free Association of German Trade Unions

1905
- Russian Revolution, Soviets in St. Petersburg
- Controversy in SPD over mass strike

1906
- Mannheim Agreement between SPD and the Free Trade Unions aims at reformist goals, rejects general strike

1912
- SPD membership over 1 million, receives four and one-half million votes and 110 seats in the Reichstag

1914
- World War begins; SPD and trade unions agree to Civil Peace

1915
- Clandestine beginnings of the Revolutionary Shop Stewards movement in Berlin factories

1916
- May—Spartacists organize anti-war rally in Berlin, Karl Liebknecht arrested
- June—55,000 strike in Berlin for Liebknecht, against war
- December—Auxiliary War Service Act militarizes German labor

1917
- April—Some 300,000 strike in Berlin for rations, peace, civil liberties
- November—Bolshevik Revolution in Russia

1918
- January—500,000 strike in Berlin for peace, food and democracy
- March—Treaty of Brest-Litovsk with Soviet Russia
- October—Constitutional monarchy declared, Social Democrats enter government
- Joint labor-management national agreement for post-war co-operation
- November—Revolt in the navy, revolution, fall of the monarchy, councils take power in localities
- Republic proclaimed
- Council of People's Representatives formed with an SPD majority; SPD and military secretly agree on suppression of social revolution
- Armistice
- Zentralarbeitsgemeinschaft accord between business and labor
- December— National Congress of Councils in Berlin
- USPD quits Council of People's Representatives

Appendix A

1919
- January —Founding of KPD
- Spartacus Uprising
- Elections to National Assembly
- February—Friedrich Ebert assumes presidency of the Weimar Republic
- April—Council republic in Munich
- June —Versailles Peace Treaty
- August —Weimar constitution, Article 165 provides for works councils in industry
- December—Founding of FAUD

1920
- January—Factory Council Law
- AAUD founded
- March—Kapp Putsch and general strike
- April—KAPD founded

1921
- March—March Action led by the KPD

Appendix B

Abbreviations

AAUD—Allgemeine Arbeiter-Union Deutschlands

AAUD-E—Allgemeine Arbeiter-Union Deutschlands—Einheitsorganisation

ADGB—Allgemeiner Deutscher Gewerkschaftbund

CGT—Confederation General du Travail

CNT—Confederacion Nacional de Trabajo

DMV—Deutsche Metallarbeiter Verband

FAUD—Freie Arbeiter-Union Deutschland

FVdG—Freie Vereinigung deutscher Gewerkschaften

IWW—Industrial Workers of the World

KAPD—Kommunistische Arbeiter-Partei Deutschlands

KPD—Kommunistische Partei Deutschlands

RO—Revolutionaere Obleute

SDP—Sozialdemokratische Partei Deutschlands

USPD—Unabhaengige Sozialdemokratische Partei Deutschlands

Bibliography

Anweiler, Oscar. 1974. *The Soviets: The Russian Workers, Peasants, and Soldiers Councils, 1905-1921*. New York: Pantheon Books.

Arnold, Volker. 1985. *Raetebewegung und Raetetheorien in der Novemberrevolution*. Hamburg: Junius Verlag.

Bailey, Stephen. 1980. "The Berlin Strike of January 1918." *Central European History*. (Atlanta—Emory University). Vol. XII, No. 2 - June, pp. 158-174.

Berger, Stefan. 1995. "Germany," in Stefan Berger and David Broughton, eds., *The Force of Labour: The Western European Labour Movement and the Working Class in the Twentieth Century*. Oxford and Washington D.C.: Berg, pp. 71-105.

Berlin—Wie Es War. (1932) 1985. International Historic Films (Chicago). VRS video. 87 minutes.

Bieber, Hans-Joachim. 1987. "The Socialist Trade Unions in War and Revolution, 1914-1919," in Roger Fletcher, ed., *Bernstein to Brandt: A Short History of German Social Democracy*. London: Edward Arnold, pp. 74-85.

Bock, Hans Manfred. 1969. *Syndikalismus und Linkskommunismus von 1918-1923*. Meisenheim am Glan: Verlag Anton Hain.

Bock, Hans Manfred. 1990. "Anarchosyndicalism in the German Labour Movement: A Rediscovered Minority Tradition," in Marcel van der Linden and Wayne Thorpe, eds. *Revolutionary Syndicalism: an International Perspective*. Aldershot, UK and Brookfield, VT: Scolar Press, pp. 59-79.

Brendel, Cajo. 1973. "N. Lenin als Stratege der Burgerliche Revolution." *Schwarze Protokolle*. (Berlin). N. 4 - April, pp. 14-45.

Bricianer, Serge. 1978. *Pannekoek and the Workers Councils*. St. Louis: Telos Press.

Brigl-Mathis, Kurt. (1926) 1978. "Die soziologischen Grundlagen des Betriebsraetegesetzen" in R. Crusis, G. Schiefelbein and M. Wilke, eds., *Die Betriebsraete in der Weimarer Republik, V.II.* Berlin: Verlag Olle & Wolter, pp. 1-43.

Brock, Adolf. 1978. ""Die Arbeiter- und Soldatenraete von der revolutionaeren Aktion zur Integration" in R. Crusius, G. Schiefelbein and M. Wilke, eds., *Die Betriebsraete in der Weimarer Republik, V.I.* Berlin: Verlag Olle & Wolter, pp. 9-43.

Bruck, W.F. 1962. *Social and Economic History of Germany from William II to Hitler, 1888-1939.* New York: Russell & Russell.

Carsten, F.L. 1972. *Revolution in Central Europe 1918-1919.* Berkeley and Los Angeles: University of California Press.

Carsten, F.L. 1982. *War Against War: British and German Radical Movements in the First World War.* Berkeley and Los Angeles: University of California Press.

Comfort, Richard A. 1966. *Revolutionary Hamburg: Labor Politics in the Early Weimar Republic.* Stanford: Stanford University Press.

Daumig, Ernst (1918) 1971. "Nationalversammlung oder Raetesystem?" in Guenter Hillman, ed., *Die Raetebewegung, V.I.* Reinbek bei Hamburg: Rowohlt, pp. 82-87.

Daumig, Ernst. (1919) 1969a. "Raetesystem—Nationalversammlung—Verfassungs-entwurf," in Dieter Schneider and Rudolf Kuda, eds., *Arbeiterraete in der Novemberrevolution: Ideen, Wirkung, Documente.* Frankfurt am Main: Suhrkamp Verlag, pp. 94-95.

Daumig, Ernst. (1920) 1969b. "Die Raetegedanke und sein Verwirklichung" in Dieter Schneider and Rudolf Kuda, eds., *Arbeiterraete in Novemberrevolution: Ideen, Wirkung, Documente.* Frankfurt am Main: Suhrkamp Verlag, pp. 69-76.

Diesel, Eugen. 1931. *Germany and the Germans.* New York: Macmillan.

Domansky, Elisabeth. 1989. ""The rationalization of class struggle: strikes and strike strategy of the German Metalworkers' Union, 1891-1922", in Leopold H. Haimson and Charles Tilly, eds. *Strikes, wars, and revolutions in an international perspective.* Cambridge: Cambridge University Press, pp. 321-355.

Eley, Geoff. 1984. "Combining Two Histories: The SPD and the German Working Class Before 1914." *Radical History Review* (New York). Nos. 28-30 -September, pp. 13-44.

Eley, Geoff. 1987. "The SPD in War and Revolution, 1914-1919," in Roger Fletcher, ed., *Bernstein to Brandt: A Short History of German Social Democracy*. London: Edward Arnold, pp. 65-74.

Eyck, Eric. 1967. *A History of the Weimar Republic, Vol. I*. New York: Wiley & Sons.

Franck, Harry A. 1920. *Vagabonding Through Changing Germany*. New York: Grosset & Dunlap.

Freie Arbeiter Union. 1986. *Anarcho-Syndikalismus in Deutschland*. Munich: FAU/IAA pamphlet.

Frolich, Paul. (1939) 1972. *Rosa Luxemburg: Ideas in Action*. London: Pluto Press.

Gay, Peter. 1962. *The Dilemma of Democratic Socialism: Eduard Bernstein's Challenge to Marx*. New York: Collier Books.

Geary, Dick. 1978. "Radicalism and the Workers: Metalworkers and the Revolution 1914-23," in Richard J. Evans, ed., *Society and Politics in Wilhelmine Germany*. London and New York: Croom Helm/ Barnes & Noble Books, pp. 267-286.

Geary, Dick. 1981. *European Labour Protest 1848-1939*. London: Methuen.

Geary, Dick. 1982. "Identifying Militancy: The Assessment of Workingclass Attitudes toward State and Society," in Richard J. Evans, ed., *The German Working Class 1888-1933*. London and Totowa, NJ: Croom Helm/Barnes & Noble Books, pp. 220-246.

Geary, Dick. 1987. "Working Class Culture in Imperial Germany," in Roger Fletcher, ed., *Bernstein to Brandt: A Short History of German Social Democracy*. London: Edward Arnold, pp. 11-16.

Gerber, John. 1988. "Anton Pannekeok and Emancipatory Socialism," in *New Politics* (Brooklyn). Vol. II, No. 1 (New Series) - Summer, pp. 119-130.

Gerhard, H.W. (1931) 1972. "Der Anarchosyndikalismus in Deutschland," in Augustin Souchy, ed., *Geschichte der Internationalen Arbeiter Assoziation von 1921-1931*. Hamburg: MAD Verlag, pp. 50-53.

Geyer, Kurt. (1919) 1969. "Sozialismus und Raetesystem," in Dieter Schneider and Rudolf Kuda, eds., *Arbeiterraete in der Novemberrevolution: Ideen, Wirkungen, Documente*. Frankfurt am Main: Suhrkamp Verlag, pp. 78-80.

Gill, Anton. 1993. *A Dance Between Flames: Berlin Between the Wars*. New York: Carroll & Graf.

Gluckstein, Donny: 1985. *The Western Soviets: Workers Councils versus Parliament, 1915-1920*. London: Bookmarks.

Gorter, Hermann. (1920) 1967. "Open Letter to Comrade Lenin" in Helmut Gruber, ed., *International Communism in the Era of Lenin: A Documentary History*. Ithaca: Cornell University Press, pp. 231-240.

Gruber, Helmut. 1967. "The German March Action" in Helmut Gruber, ed., *International Communism in the Era of Lenin: A Documentary History*. Ithaca: Cornell University Press, pp. 312-319.

Haffner, Sebastian. 1986. *Failure of a Revolution: Germany 1918-1919*. Chicago: Banner Press.

Hagerty, Thomas J. (1905) 1968. "Father Hagerty's 'Wheel of Fortune'," in Joyce L. Kornbluth, ed., *Rebel Voices: An IWW Anthology*. Ann Arbor: University of Michigan Press, pp.10-11.

Hamerow, Theodore S. 1972. *Restoration, Revolution, Reaction: Economics and Politics in Germany, 1815-1871*. Princeton: Princeton University Press.

Hamerow, Theodore S. 1985. "Bismarck and the Emergence of the Social Question in Germany," in Volker Durr, Kathy Harms and Peter Hayes, eds., *Imperial Germany*. Madison and London: University of Wisconsin Press, pp. 17-31.

Horn, Daniel. 1969. *The German Naval Mutinies of World War I*. New Brunswick: Rutgers University Press.

Ihlau, Olaf. 1971. *Die roten Kampfer: Ein Betrag zur Geschichte der Arbeiterbewegung in der Weimarer Republik und im Dritten Reich*. Erlangen: Verlag Politladen.

Institut fur Marxismus-Leninismus. 1968. *Illustrierte Geschichte der Novemberrevolution in Deutschland*. Berlin: Dietz Verlag.

Kessler, Harry. (1918-1937) 1971. *In the Twenties: The Diaries of Harry Kessler*. New York, Chicago and San Francisco: Holt, Reinhart and Winston.

Kluge, Ulrich. 1985. *Die deutsche Revolution 1918/1919*. Frankfurt am Main: Suhrkamp.

Kolb, Eberhard. 1962. *Die Arbeiterrate in der deutschen Innenpolitik, 1918- 1919*. Dusseldorf: Droste Verlag.

Kommunistische Partei Deutschlands (Spartakusbund). (1919) 1971. "Alle Macht den Arbeiter- und Soldatenraeten" in Guenter Hillman, ed., *Die Raetebewegung, V. I*. Reinbek bei Hamburg: Rowohlt, 97-99.

Landau, Kurt. (1937) 1992. "The Spanish Revolution of 1936 and the German Revolution of 1918-19." *Revolutionary History* (London). Vol. 4, Nos. 1/2 - Winter, pp. 73-99.

Landes, David S. 1969. *The Unbound Prometheus: Technological Change and Industrial Development in Western Europe from 1750 to the Present*. Cambridge: Cambridge University Press.

Lenin, V.I. (1902) 1972. "What Is to Be Done?," in Helmut Gruber, ed., *International Communism in the Era of Lenin*. Ithaca: Cornell University Press, pp. 25-39.

Lenin, V.I. (1920) 1969. *Left-Wing Communism: An Infantile Disorder*. Peking: Foreign Languages Press.

Lewin-Dorsch, Eugen. (1919) 1971. ""Fuehrer und Massen," in Guenter Hillman, ed., *Die Raetebewegung, V. I.* Reinbek bei Hamburg: Rowohlt, pp. 128-133.

Lidtke, Vernon L. 1985. *The Alternative Culture: Socialist Labor in Imperial Germany*. New York and Oxford: Oxford University Press.

Lorwin, Val. 1954. *The French Labor Movement*. Cambridge, MA: Harvard University Press.

Luxemburg, Rosa. (1904/1918) 1970. *The Russian Revolution/Leninism or Marxism*. Ann Arbor: University of Michigan Press.

Luxemburg, Rosa (1906/1915) 1971. *The Mass Strike, the Political Party, and the Trade Unions/The Junius Pamphlet*. New York: Harper & Row.

Lynd, Staughton. 1997. *Living Inside Our Hope: A Steadfast Radical's Thoughts on Rebuilding the Movement*. Ithaca and London: Cornell University Press.

Masur, Gerhard. 1970. *Imperial Berlin*. New York: Dorset Press.

Mattick, Paul. 1975. "Anti-Bolshevist Communism in Germany." *Telos* (St. Louis—Washington University). No. 26 - Winter, pp. 57-69.

Mattick, Paul. 1978. *Anti-Bolshevik Communism*. London: Merlin Press.

Mattick, Paul. 1983. *Marxism: Last Refuge of the Bourgeoisie?* Armonk, NY and London: M.E. Sharpe/Merlin Press.

McGuffie, Chris. 1985. *Working in Metal: Management and Labour in the Metal Industries of Europe and the USA, 1890-1914*. London: Merlin Press.

Meijer, H. Canne. (1938) 1972. *The Origins of the Movement of Workers Councils in Germany 1918-29*. Montreal: Our Generation pamphlet.

Michels, Robert. (1915) 1962. *Political Parties: A Sociological Study of the Oligarchical Tendencies of Modern Democracy*. New York: Collier Books.
Miller, Susanne and Heinrich Potthoff. 1983. *A History of German Social Democracy: From 1848 to the Present*. Leamington Spa, Hamburg and New York: Berg.
Mitchell, David. 1970. *1919: Red Mirage*. New York: Macmillan.
Mitchell, Harvey and Peter N. Stearns. 1971. *The European Labor Movement, the Working Classes and the Origins of Social Democracy 1890-1914*. Itasca, IL: Peacock Publishers.
Morgan, David W. 1975. *The Socialist Left and the German Revolution: A History of the German Independent Social Democratic Party, 1917-1922*. Ithaca and London: Cornell University Press.
Morgan, David W. 1982. "Ernst Daumig and the German Revolution of 1918," *Central European History* (Atlanta—Emory University), Vol. XV, No. 4 - December, pp. 303-331.
Moses, John A. 1982. *Trade Unionism in Germany from Bismarck to Hitler, 1869-1933, Vols. I & II*. London: George Prior Publishers.
Muller, Richard. (1919) 1969a. "Forderungen fur die Raeteverfassung" in Dieter Schneider and Rudolf Kuda, eds. *Arbeiterraete in der Novemberrevolution: Ideen, Wirkung, Documente*. Frankfurt am Main: Suhrkamp Verlag, pp. 84-86.
Muller, Richard. (1919) 1969b. "Hie Gewerkschaft! Hie Betriebsorganization!," in Dieter Schneider and Rudolf Kuda, eds., *Arbeiterraete in der Novemberrevolution: Ideen, Wirkung, Documente*. Frankfurt am Main: Suhrkamp Verlag, pp. 99-102.
Muller, Richard. (1921) 1969c. "Demokratie oder Raetesystem," in Dieter Schneider and Rudolf Kuda, eds., *Arbeiterraete in der Novemberrevolution: Ideen, Wirkungen, Documente*. Frankfurt am Main: Suhrkamp Verlag, pp. 91-94.
Muller, Richard. (1921) 1970. *1918: Raete in Deutschland*. Osnabruck: Kommunikation Zentrum pamphlet.
Muller, Richard. (1924) 1971a. "Revolutionaere Gymnastik" in Guenter Hillman, ed., *Die Raetebewegung, V.I*. Reinbek bei Hamburg: Rowohlt, pp. 21-24.
Muller, Richard. (1925) 1971b. *Die Novemberrevolution*. West Berlin: Olle & Walter.
Nettl, Peter. 1969. *Rosa Luxemburg*. London, Oxford and New York: Oxford University Press.

Nolan, Mary. 1986. "Economic Crisis, State Policy, and Working Class Formation in Germany, 1870-1900," in Ira Katznelson and Aristide R. Zolberg, eds., *Working Class Formation: Nineteenth Century Patterns in Western Europe and the United States*. Princeton: Princeton University Press, pp. 384-500.

Opel, Fritz. 1980. *Der Deutsche Metallarbeiter-Verband wahrend des ersten Weltkrieges und der Revolution*. Koln: Bund-Verlag.

Pannekoek, Anton. (1942) 1975. "Workers Councils," in Jeremy Brecher, Rick Burns, Elizabeth Long, Paul Mattick jr. and Peter Rachleff, eds., *Root & Branch: The Rise of the Workers Movements*. Greenwich, CT: Fawcett Crest, pp. 384-500.

Pannekoek, Anton and Herman Gorter. (1912-1921) 1978. In D.A. Smart, ed., *Pannekoek and Gorter's Marxism*. London: Pluto Press.

Patch, William L. 1984. "German Social History and Labor History: A Troubled Partnership," *The Journal of Modern History* (University of Chicago), Vol. 56, No. 3 - September, pp. 483-498.

Peltz, William A. 1987. *The Spartakusbund and the German Working Class Movement*. Lewiston, NY and Queenston, Ontario: Edwin Mellen Press.

Peterson, Brian. 1975. "Workers Councils in Germany, 1918-19: Recent Literature on the Ratebewegung," *New German Critique* (Milwaukee—University of Wisconsin), No. 4 - Winter, pp. 113-124.

Peukert, Detlev J.K. 1992. *The Weimar Republic: The Crisis of Classical Modernity*. New York: Hill & Wang.

Pliever, Theodore. 1981. *Der Kaiser ging, die Generale blieben*. Frankfurt am Main: Fischer Taschenbuch Verlag.

Regler, Gustav. 1959. *The Owl of Minerva*. New York: Farrar, Straus and Cudahy.

Reichenbach, Bernard. (1969) 1994. "The KAPD in Retrospect," *Revolutionary History* (London), Vol. 5, No. 2 - Spring, pp. 137-144.

Riesel, Rene. 1981. "Preliminaries on the Councils and Councilist Organization," in Ken Knabb, ed., *Situationist International Anthology*. Berkeley: Bureau of Public Secrets, pp. 270-282.

Roberts, James S. 1982. "Drink and the Labour Movement: the Schnaps Boycott of 1909," in Richard J. Evans, ed., *The German Working Class 1888-1933*. London and Totowa, NJ: Croon Helm/Barnes & Noble, pp. 80-107.

Rocker, Rudolph. 1938. *Anarcho-Syndicalism*. London: Seecker and Warburg.

Rocker, Rudolph. (1948) 1985. *Ein Leben fur den Revolutionaren Syndikalismus: Biographie von Fritz Kater*. Hamburg: Verlag Folkert Mohrhof pamphlet.

Rosenberg, Arthur. (1961) 1994. "The Kapp Putsch and the Working Class," *Revolutionary History* (London), Vol. 5, No. 2 - Spring, pp. 37-41.

Rosenhaft, Eve. 1982. "Organizing the 'Lumpenproletariat': Cliques and Communists in Berlin during the Weimar Republic," in Richard J. Evans, ed., *The German Working Class 1888-1933*. London and Totowa, NJ: Croon Helm/Barnes & Noble, pp. 174-219.

Roth, Gunther. 1963. *The Social Democrats in Imperial Germany*. Totowa, NJ: Croon Helm.

Roth, Karl-Heinz. 1977. *Die 'Andere' Arbeiterbewegung und die Entwicklung der kapitalischen Repression von 1880 bis zur Gegenwart*. Munich: Bund-Verlag.

Roy, N. 1970. *Spartakism to National Bolshevism: The KPD 1918-24*. Aberdeen: Solidarity pamphlet.

Ruhle, Otto. (1924) 1974. *From the Bourgeois to the Proletarian Revolution*. Dumbarton, Scotland and London: Socialist Reproduction pamphlet.

Schneider, Dieter and Rudolf Kuda. 1969. "Arbeiterraete in der Novemberrevolution," in Dieter Schneider and Rudolf Kuda, eds., *Arbeiterrate in der Novemberrevolution: Ideen, Wirkungen, Documente*. Frankfurt am Main: Suhrkamp Verlag, pp. 7-52.

Schneider, Michael. 1991. *A Brief History of the German Trade Unions*. Bonn: Verlag J.H.W. Dietz Nachf.

Schoenhoven, Klaus. "The Socialist Trade Unions in the Weimar Republic" in Roger Fletcher, ed., *Bernstein to Brandt: A Short History of German Social Democracy*. London: Edward Arnold, pp. 123-132.

Schorske, Carl E. 1972. *German Social Democracy, 1905-1917: The Development of the Great Schism*. New York: Harper & Row.

Shipway, Mark. 1987. "Council Communism," in Maximilien Rubel and John Crump, eds., *Non-Market Socialism in the Nineteenth and Twentieth Centuries*. London: Macmillan.

Souchy, Agustin. 1976. Interview with the author. Cambridge, MA, August 18-19.

Souchy, Augustin. 1992. *Beware Anarchist! A Life for Freedom: An Autobiography*. Chicago: Charles H. Kerr.

Steenson, Gary. 1981. *Not One Man! Not One Penny! German Social Democracy, 1863-1914.* Pittsburgh: U. of Pittsburgh Press.

Steinmetz, George. 1991. "Workers and the Welfare State in Imperial Germany," *International Labor and Working Class History* (New York—New School for Social Research), No. 40 - Fall, pp. 18-46.

Taylor, Simon. 1986. *Germany 1918-1933.* London: Duckworth.

Tegel, Susan. 1987. "The SPD in Imperial Germany, 1871-1914," in Roger Fletcher, ed., *Bernstein to Brandt: A Short History of German Social Democracy.* London: Edward Arnold, pp. 16-24.

Ten Broke, K. 1988. "Theodore Pliever: Leben und Werk," *Direckte Aktion* (Hamburg), N. 71 - September/October, pp. 20-22.

Trotnow, Helmut. 1984. *Karl Liebknecht (1871-1919): A Political Biography.* Hamden, CT: Archon Books.

Trotsky, Leon. (1922) 1971. *1905.* New York: Vintage Books.

Ullrich, Volker. 1987. "Everyday Life and the German Working Class, 1914-1918," in Roger Fletcher, ed., *Bernstein to Brandt: A Short History of German Social Democracy.* London: Edward Arnold, pp. 55-64.

Umbreit, Paul. (1920) 1978. "Die Aufgaben der Betriebsraete" in R. Crusis, G. Schiefelbein and M. Wilke, eds., *Die Betriebsraete in der Weimarer Republik, V.I.* Berlin: Verlag Olle & Wolter, pp. 178-179.

Von Oertzen, Peter. 1963. *Betriebsraete in der Novemberrevolution.* Dusseldorf: Droste Verlag.

Waite, Robert G.L. 1969. *Vanguard of Nazism: The Free Corps Movement in Postwar Germany 1918-1923.* New York: W.W. Norton.

Watt, Richard M. 1968. *The Kings Depart—The Tragedy of Germany: Versailles and the German Revolution.* New York: Simon and Schuster.

Winter, J.M. 1993. "Paris, London, Berlin: Capital Cities at War, 1914-1920," *International Labor and Working Class History* (New York—New School for Social Research), No. 44 - Fall, pp. 106-118.

Index

A

AAUD. *See* Allgemeine Arbeiter Union Deutschlands
AAUD-E. *See* Allgemeine Arbeiter Union Deutschlands' Einheitsorganisation
ADGB. *See* Allgemeiner Deutscher Gewerkschaftbund
AEG. *See* Allgemeine Elektrizitat Gesellschaft
Allgemeine Arbeiter Union Deutschlands, 70–71, 73, 79, 81
Allgemeine Arbeiter Union Deutschlands' Einheitsorganisation, 81
Allgemeine Elektrizitat Gesellschaft, 4
Allgemeiner Deutscher Gewerkschaftbund, 21–22, 25, 28, 32, 34, 39, 41–42, 48–49, 59–60, 66, 72, 77, 81
American manufacturing processes, 5
Anti-Bolshevik Communist Workers Party, 1
Anti-Socialist Law, 11, 22, 77
Anweiler, Oscar, 50
Apprenticeships, 9
Arbeiter-Zeitung, 28
Arbeiterpolitik, 28–29
Arnold, Volker, 5, 28, 34, 38, 48, 59, 62, 70, 72
Association of Berlin Engineering Manufacturers, 33
Association of German Iron and Steel Manufacturers, 48
Auxiliary Service Law, 35, 61
Auxiliary War Service Act, 32, 78

B

Bailey, Stephen, 40–41
Barth, Emil, 46–47
Bebel, August, 15–16
Beiersdorf, Franz, 54
Berger, Stefan, 11, 21, 23
Berlin Industrial Exposition, 4
Bernstein, Eduard, 15, 28, 32
Bieber, Hans-Joachim, 32
Bismarck, Chancellor, 10–11, 14
Bock, Hans Manfred, 16–18, 23–25, 28–29, 36, 38, 56, 69–73
Bolshevism, 1, 39, 46, 48, 71
Brendel, Cajo, 71
Brest-Litovsk Treaty, 39, 78
Brigl-Mathis, Kurt, 67–68
Brock, Adolf, 38
Bruck, W.F, 4–5
Burgfrieden, 31–32, 34–35, 78
Busch, Zirkus, 45–46

C

Carsten, F.L., 31–34, 38–41, 46, 49–50, 58
Central Association of the Employ-

ees of Germany
Central Education Commission, 13
CGT. *See* Confederation General du Travail
Charter of Amiens, 28
The Civil Peace. *See* Burgfrieden
Cohen, Adolph, 37, 39, 48
Comfort, Richard A, 44
Communism, councils, 69–74
Communist Party of Germany, 53, 71–72
Communist Workers Party, 1, 70–71
Confederacion Nacional de Trabajo, 1, 81
Confederation General du Travail, 28, 81
Council of People's Representatives, 46, 78
Councils, 37–42

D
Daumig, Ernst, 50, 53, 56–57, 59, 67
Deutsche Metallarbeiter Verband, 25–28, 37, 39, 61–63, 77, 81
Diesel, Eugen, 3–4, 7–8, 10
Dissman, Robert, 62
Dittman, Wilhelm, 47
DMV. *See* Deutsche Metallarbeiter Verband
Domansky, Elisabeth, 24–28

E
Ebert, Friedrich, 15, 28, 40, 45–46, 49–51, 53, 55, 58, 60, 65–66, 79
Eichorn, Emil, 53
Die Einigkeit, 28
Eley, Geoff, 13
Engels, Frederick, 13, 16
The Engineer. See Die Pionier
Eyck, Eric, 46, 66

F
Factory Council Law, 65, 79
FAUD. *See* Free Labor Union of Germany
Fordism, 4
Franck, Harry A., 49, 55
Franco, General, 1
Free Association of German Trade Unions, 25, 69, 77
Free Corp. *See* Freikorp
Free Labor Union of Germany, 69–70, 73, 79, 81
Free Trade Unions, 21–22, 25, 28, 32, 34, 39, 41–42, 48–49, 59–60, 66, 72, 77, 81. *See also* Trade unions
Frei Korps, 51, 58
Freie Arbeiter Union, 25, 69–70, 73, 79, 81
Freie Vereingung deutscher Gewerkschaften. *See* Free Association of German Trade Unions
Freie Vereinigung deutscher Gewerkschaften, 25, 28, 69, 81
Freikorp, 55, 58, 66
French Confederation General du Travail, 28
Friedeberg, Dr. Raphael, 16–17
Frolich, Paul, 32, 53, 55
FVdG. *See* Free Association of German Trade Unions; Freie Vereinigung deutscher Gewerkschaften

G
Gay, Peter, 12, 15
Geary, Dick, 16, 20, 22, 26, 35
General Commission of the ADGB, 22, 49
General Commission of the Free Trade Unions, 28
General Confederation of Labor. *See*

French Confederation General du Travail
General Workers Union of Germany. *See* Allgemeine Arbeiter Union Deutschlands
Gerhard, H.W., 70
German Communist Party, 53, 71–72
German Congress of Workers and Soldiers Councils, 50
German Metal Workers Union, 25–28, 37, 39, 61–63, 77, 81
German Social Democracy, 8, 11–20
Geyer, Kurt, 44
Gill, Anton, 3, 7, 34
Gluckstein, Donny, 37–42, 44, 46–50, 54
Gorter, Hermann, 19, 71–72
Groener, General Wilhelm, 46, 50–51
Gruber, Helmut, 72

H
Haffner, Sebastian, 43, 45–46, 50–51, 53–54, 58
Hamerow, Theodore S., 10, 14
Hierarchies, 24, 26, 28–29, 34, 43, 48–49
Hindenburg Line, 43
Hoelz, Max, 72
Horn, Daniel, 36, 41, 43

I
Imperial Trade Act, 8
Independent Socialist Party. *See* Unabhaengige Sozialdemokratische Partei Deutschlands
Independent Socialist Party of Germany, 32, 41, 46–47, 50, 53, 55, 62, 65–67, 78, 81
Independent Socialist Reichstag delegation, 40

Independent Works Council, 61
Industrial Workers of the World, 28, 69, 81
Institut fur Marxismus-Leninismus, 33
Intellectuals, 11, 28, 41, 56, 75–76
IWW. *See* Industrial Workers of the World

J
Die Jungen, 16

K
KAPD. *See* Kommunistische Arbeiter-Partei Deutschlands
Kapp, Wolfgang, 66, 79
Kater, Fritz, 25, 56
Kessler, Count Harry, 45, 58, 66
Kluge, Ulrich, 43–44
Koester, Fritz, 28
Kolb, Eberhard, 44, 55
Kommunistische Arbeiter-Partei Deutschlands, 1, 70–73, 79, 81
Kommunistische Partei Deutschlands, 53, 55, 70–72, 79, 81
Kommunistischen Arbeiter-Partei Deutschlands, 70

L
Landes, David, 4–5, 9
Landesburg, Dr. Otto, 47
Left-Wing Communism: An Infantile Disorder, 71
Legien, Carl, 22, 28, 32, 59, 66
Lenin, Vladimir Ilyich, 1, 71
Leninist theory, 1, 71, 75
Lichtstrahlen, 28
Lidtke, Vernon L., 12–13, 19
Liebknecht, Karl, 31–32, 34, 38, 41, 53, 55, 78
Lightrays. *See* Lichtstrahlen
Lockouts, 22, 27

Loewe Machine Tool Plant, 4
Lorwin, Val, 28
Ludendorff, General Erich, 39, 43
Luxemburg, Rosa, 17-20, 23, 28, 31-32, 41, 53, 55
Lynd, Staughton, 76

M
Majority Social Democrats, 46, 55, 76
Mannheim Agreement, 22-23, 77
March Action, 72, 79
Marx, Karl, 13-14, 71
Marxism, 15, 33, 47
Marxist revisionism, 76
Marxist theory, 2, 22, 28, 70
Masur, Gerhard, 3-5, 8, 10, 33-34
Mattick, Paul, 1, 71, 73, 75
May Day celebrations, 17, 26, 76
McGuffie, Chris, 8-10
Meijer, H. Canne, 70-73
Metal Workers News. See Metall-Arbeiter-Zeitung
Metall-Arbeiter-Zeitung, 62
Michels, Robert, 15
Milkuschutz, Gustav, 47
Miller, Susanne, 8, 11-12, 14, 16, 21, 31-32, 45, 55, 66
Mitchell, David, 14
Morgan, David W., 32, 41, 53-54, 56-57, 60, 62-63, 65-67, 69, 72
Moses, John A., 32-33, 43, 59, 61, 63
Muller, Richard, 37-41, 44, 46, 48-50, 53, 55, 59, 62-63, 67
Munz Street Center, 67

N
Neue Zeit, 24
New Times. See Neue Zeit
Nolan, Mary, 9, 12
Noske, Gustav, 51, 57-58, 60, 62, 65

O
Obleute. *See* Revolutionaere Obleute
Opel, Fritz, 26-27, 39-40, 59-63

P
Pannekoek, Anton, 18-19, 73
Parliamentarianism, 17
People's Naval Division, 46, 50, 54, 57
Peukert, Detlev J.K., 3
Die Pionier, 9, 28
Polish Solidarity union, 76
Prussia, 3

R
Regler, Gustav, 51
Reich Chancellory, 45
Reichenbach, Bernard, 70, 73
Reichert, Jakob, 48
Retzlaw, Karl, 35
Revolutionaere Obleute, 37, 39, 45, 50, 56, 81
Revolutionary Committee, 53-55
Revolutionary Shop Stewards. *See* Revolutionaere Obleute
Riesel, Rene, 71
RO. *See* Revolutionaere Obleute
Roberts, James S., 12, 20
Rocker, Rudolf, 16, 25, 69
Rosenhaft, Eve, 7-8
Roth, Gunther, 13
Roth, Karl-Heinz, 20
Roy, N., 70-72
Ruehle, Otto, 71
Russian Revolution, 17, 19, 39, 45, 49, 72, 77

S
Schneider, Michael, 8, 11, 21-25, 31-35, 37, 39, 46, 48-49, 56, 59-60, 72

Index

Schoenhoven, Klaus, 72
Schorske, Carl E., 14–17, 22, 24–25, 31
SDP. *See* Sozialdemokratische Partei Deutschlands
Siemens Company, 4
Sinzheimer, Hugo, 60
Social Democracy, 1, 8, 11–20, 22, 29, 57, 60, 69
Social Democratic Party, 11–12, 15, 17, 25, 28, 31–32, 41–42, 48, 50, 60, 77
Social Democrats, 10, 12, 15–16, 18–20, 22, 31, 34, 43–44, 46, 55, 58, 66, 72, 76, 78
Socialist. See Sozialist
Souchy, Augustin, 1, 56, 60, 69, 71–72
Sozialdemokratische Partei Deutschlands, 11, 41, 81
Sozialist, 28
Sozialistengesetz, 11
Spanish Civil War, 1
Spanish National Confederation of Labor, 1
Spanish Revolution, 76
Spartacist League, 34, 41–42
Spartacist Week, 55
Spartacists, 41, 53, 55, 57, 60, 72, 76, 78
SPD. *See* Sozialdemokratische Partei Deutschlands
Steenson, Gary, 12, 14, 16, 21, 23
Steinmetz, George, 10, 12

T
Taylor, Simon, 47
Taylorism, 4, 27
Tegel, Susan, 12
Trade unions, 21–30
Treaty of Brest-Litovsk, 39, 78
Treaty of Versailles, 66

Trotnow, Helmut, 32, 34
Trotsky, Leon, 17
Tsarist Russia, 18, 31, 72, 76

U
Ullrich, Volker, 34–36, 38
Umbreit, Paul, 61
Unabhaengige Sozialdemokratische Partei Deutschlands, 32, 41, 46–47, 50, 53, 55, 62, 65–67, 78, 81
Unions, 21–30
Unity. See Die Einigkeit
Urban proletariat, 7–10
USPD. *See* Unabhaengige Sozialdemokratische Partei Deutschlands

V
Versailles Treaty, 66
von Borsig, Ernst, 33
von Hindenburg, General Paul, 39
von Oertzen, Peter, 37, 41, 48, 55–56
von Raumer, Hans, 43
Vorwaerts, 20, 54, 56, 58

W
Waite, Robert G.L., 51, 54, 58, 66
Winter, J.M., 33, 35, 38
Wissell, Rudolf, 58
Workers councils, 37–42
Workers Politics. See Arbeiterpolitik
Workers' Times. See Arbeiter-Zeitung

Y
The Young Ones. *See* Die Jungen

Z
ZAG. *See* Zentralarbeitsgemeinschaft
Zentralarbeitsgemeinschaft, 49, 78

About the Author

Martin Comack was born in New York City. He received a Bachelor's degree in History from Hunter College, City University of New York, and was subsequently employed as a soldier, merchant seaman, teamster, civil servant and, more recently, adjunct professor. He holds Master's degrees from Harvard (Social Psychology) and the University of Massachusetts Amherst (Labor Studies). He received a doctorate in Political Science from Northeastern University, and has also attended the Academy of Labor and Social Relations (Moscow) and the Fundacion para la Educacion de Trabajadores (Mexico).

His articles, essays and reviews have appeared in various publications, including the *Labor Studies Journal*, *New Politics* and *CNT-Madrid*. He is also the author of the forthcoming, *Comrades and Citizens: Militant Labor Organizations and Democratization in Communist Poland and Corporate Mexico* (Edwin Mellen Press). He currently resides in the Boston area.